Introduction to SparxSystems Enterprise Architect

Documenting Enterprise Architecture in the Most Affordable Enterprise Architecture Suite

Peter Doomen

Apress®

Introduction to SparxSystems Enterprise Architect: Documenting Enterprise Architecture in the Most Affordable Enterprise Architecture Suite

Peter Doomen
Lier, Belgium

ISBN-13 (pbk): 978-1-4842-9311-9
https://doi.org/10.1007/978-1-4842-9312-6

ISBN-13 (electronic): 978-1-4842-9312-6

Managing Director, Apress Media LLC: Welmoed Spahr
Acquisitions Editor: Aditee Mirashi
Development Editor: James Markham
Coordinating Editor: Aditee Mirashi

Cover designed by eStudioCalamar

Cover image designed by Freepik (www.freepik.com)

Distributed to the book trade worldwide by Apress Media, LLC, 1 New York Plaza, New York, NY 10004, U.S.A. Phone 1-800-SPRINGER, fax (201) 348-4505, e-mail orders-ny@springer-sbm.com, or visit www.springeronline.com. Apress Media, LLC is a California LLC and the sole member (owner) is Springer Science + Business Media Finance Inc (SSBM Finance Inc). SSBM Finance Inc is a **Delaware** corporation.

For information on translations, please e-mail booktranslations@springernature.com; for reprint, paperback, or audio rights, please e-mail bookpermissions@springernature.com.

Apress titles may be purchased in bulk for academic, corporate, or promotional use. eBook versions and licenses are also available for most titles. For more information, reference our Print and eBook Bulk Sales web page at http://www.apress.com/bulk-sales.

Any source code or other supplementary material referenced by the author in this book is available to readers on GitHub (https://github.com/Apress). For more detailed information, please visit http://www.apress.com/source-code.

Printed on acid-free paper

I dedicate this book to my father, who passed away when I was at the age I first conceived the idea for this book.

Table of Contents

About the Author

Peter Doomen has been working as an architect, analyst, consultant, and teacher. He has been using Enterprise Architect since version 4. He has written two other books about the same subject. In daily life, he is fond of wine in general and champagne in particular. He likes to teach about that subject as well.

About the Technical Reviewer

Joost Van Eemeren has been a software engineer/architect for over 25 years in several industries such as digital printing, ERP, and payroll.

With a special focus on UX, architecture, and analyses, Joost has been working on both new products and modernizing large old-style architecture applications.

Acknowledgments

It has been a pleasure working with the Apress technical staff – Aditee who took care of the first contacts and Shonmirin who then took over and followed every step of the production process of this book.

Also thanks to Joost, the technical editor who provided me with helpful insights to increase the readability of the book and who detected several not easy-to-spot issues when following the steps provided in this book.

Special thanks to both Jim and Mark from Apress, who reviewed the original manuscript in more than serious depth. We totally left out Michael, which took all three of us many hours of (re)work, but none of us will regret.

It goes without saying that if you spot any errors or shortcomings, I am the only one responsible. Please let me know.

Introduction

SparxSystems Enterprise Architect (EA) has always been my "working horse," so to speak, when I had to perform serious modeling work. It might not be perfect – which tool is? But it is very reliable and full of features. In fact, it is so feature-rich that even daily users take the time to write me a message when they discover hidden gems.

I remember a meeting with five expert users where I handed out a sheet showing four little secrets – none of the other "experts" in the room knew about all four. And each of them could have written a similar cheat sheet.

Even if you can find most of these secrets in the EA manual – a manuscript of way more than 1000 pages, mostly covering simple and easy-to-guess functionalities or rarely used, very specialized stuff – all this is presented in a rather dry and mechanical way. I am not blaming technical writers at SparxSystems: it is their job to write a manual that covers the entire functional domain in a consistent way, which they invariably do.

Yet I think regular users of Enterprise Architect need something else.

In the first place, a gradual introduction to the tool "Enterprise Architect" with a clear overview of a model, the different views, and the role of elements, connectors, and diagrams. This book is built up in a logical order, going from the structure of the model, over the elements that populate it and their connections, toward the diagrams that show the contents to the outside world. Later chapters are devoted to increasing productivity and reuse.

Second, a concrete case they can relate to. Enter Systemplar, a growth-oriented company that provides products and services worldwide. They have decided to rely on SparxSystems Enterprise Architect to document their enterprise architecture. The Systemplar case shows the use of EA in real life: they have a list of business processes, software tools, strategy decks, location lists, and other stuff that will populate the Enterprise Architecture model. The book will show you exactly how to deal with external data that evolves over time.

Third, we will take the opportunity to bring together EA's features in a context so that you can easily apply it to your own. For example, we will use the "diagram legend" feature to build a heat map based on external data that indicate if a software component is functionally and technically adequate. Even if this is not an exact reflection of the challenge you are facing, you can apply the same techniques to your own world.

Although I will take my time to explain the basic concepts thoroughly and we go from basics to advanced in the latter part of the book, I fully realize we only cover a part of EA's full feature set. I don't consider this a disadvantage: on the one hand, most advanced features are only useful to a very specific subset of EA users; on the other hand, we will have put in place a sturdy base to build on. The appendix shows several places to refer to if your hunger is still great.

CHAPTER 1

Setting Up SparxSystems Enterprise Architect

SparxSystems Enterprise Architect (EA) is a logical choice for many companies and organizations: it combines a broad feature set with an affordable price. This chapter provides a quick overview of EA and concludes with downloading and installation instructions so that you are properly prepared to tackle the tasks in the chapters that follow.

Comparing the Different Versions of EA

A quick look at the SparxSystems website UML modeling tools for Business, Software, Systems, and Architecture (sparxsystems.com) reveals that there are four editions, each of which comes in two flavors (*standard* and *floating*). Furthermore, there are three products that can work together:

- Enterprise Architect is the main product of SparxSystems. It is a feature-rich UML modeling tool that supports many other languages besides UML and also allows you to create your own modeling language.

© Peter Doomen 2023
P. Doomen, *Introduction to SparxSystems Enterprise Architect*,
https://doi.org/10.1007/978-1-4842-9312-6_1

- Pro Cloud Server allows you to open up the models you create to non-EA users. For example, you can create an Enterprise Architecture model and share it with business stakeholders. They can comment on the model via a web interface so they don't need to install EA themselves.

- Prolaborate takes this collaboration a step further, making it easy to publish a part of your model and having others work on it. Also, it allows you to enable EA models in Confluence or SharePoint and to link them to items in Jira or Azure DevOps, so you can trace models to user stories.

For this book, we will need only Enterprise Architect.

Editions of EA

The simplest version of EA is the Professional edition, which is suited for working alone or in small teams on a project.

When the team grows, you will want to step up to the Corporate edition. This version allows you to create a central repository in SQL Server or Oracle so that a large number of people can work on a project without causing locks. Also, the Corporate edition has improved communication tools such as model mail and chat.

The Unified edition adds features that allow you to simulate models and to create software code from models. It also adds enterprise frameworks such as TOGAF.

The most complete edition is called the Ultimate edition. It offers MDG integration with MS Office and row-level security so you can fine-tune access to parts of the model.

For this book, we will need only the Professional version of EA, which is already feature-rich.

Flavors of EA

The standard flavor is suited when you need a personal license that cannot be shared with others. For example, if you are a consultant who works with EA day in, day out, you might want your own license.

The floating flavor is preferred when you have a team that occasionally works with EA. Each time a user opens EA, a key is reserved. When you close the EA interface, the key is released again. There are three ways to implement this: file based, via the Keystore Service, or via the Floating License Server (only via the Pro Cloud Server).

For this book, we will use a standard version of EA, although it really doesn't matter if you use a floating license.

Downloading and Setting Up EA

When you buy a license for EA, SparxSystems or their retailer for your region will send you an email with the details on how to download and install EA. *Note: Since version 16, EA is available for 64-bit architectures as well as for 32-bit architectures. Make sure to download the correct one: the functionality is the same, but performance will suffer if you run a 32-bit version on a 64-bit architecture.*

Follow these steps:

1. Click the link to the Registered User Area.

2. A dialog window appears – fill in your UserID and password.

3. In the Registered User Area, click Registered Downloads (Figure 1-1).

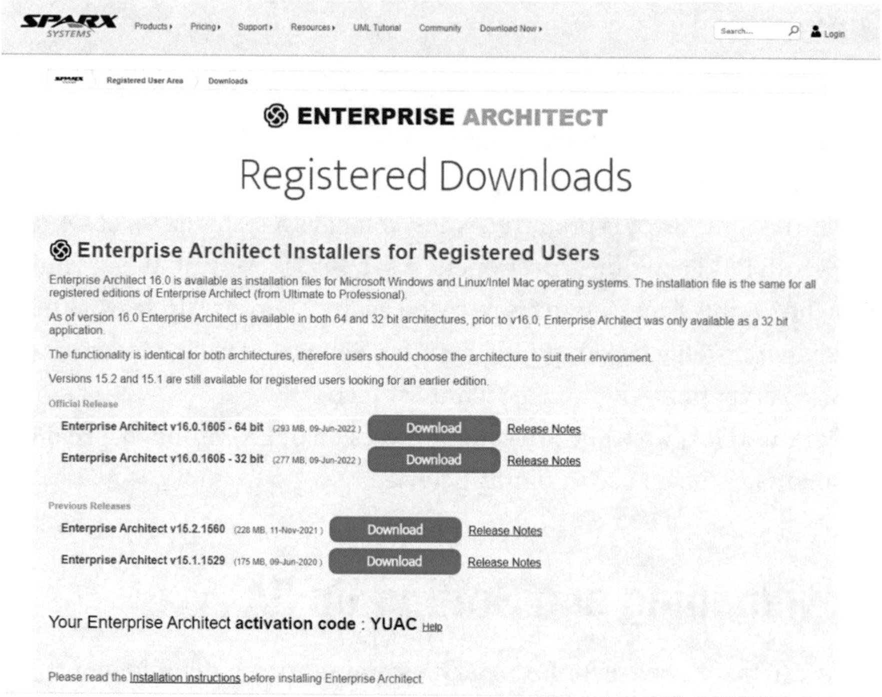

Figure 1-1. *Registered User Area*

4. In the Registered Downloads section, you can download the newest version of EA. This could be a beta version, but you can always download a previous, "stable" release. In this same section, there are detailed instructions for when you want to set up user security or a DBMS repository.

5. After installing EA on your machine, start the application. The License Management window will appear where you can add the key you received via email (Figure 1-2).

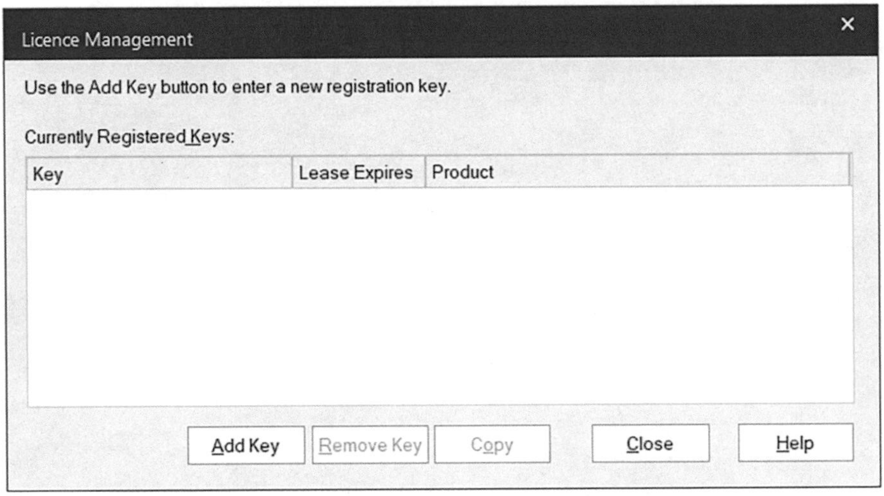

Figure 1-2. *Add your key here*

6. The last step is to enter the activation code, a four-
    letter code that you can get from the Registered User
    Area and in the email that was sent to you. After
    having agreed with the Terms of Use, you can finally
    start working with EA.

Summary

In this brief chapter, you received a crash course on EA and went through
the installation steps to ensure your computer is set up correctly. The next
chapter offers an overview of the Big Five of Enterprise Architect: models,
elements, connectors, packages, and diagrams. It will also introduce the
Zachman Framework, a simple but effective framework for documenting
enterprise architectures.

CHAPTER 2

The First Model: Documenting the Systemplar Enterprise Architecture

In this chapter, you'll prepare a detailed plan for an enterprise architecture that will fit a company's (Systemplar) needs as it grows. This is a multilayered process that requires keen attention to several moving parts. We'll start with a high-level review of the plan and a potential model to follow, the Zachman Framework. This will provide the necessary background for the matter at hand.

We'll then turn our attention to the central concepts of Enterprise Architect: repositories and projects, the Model Wizard, packages, diagrams, elements, and connectors. All of these will be key factors to document the Systemplar Enterprise Architecture. So, without further ado, let's dive into our first case.

© Peter Doomen 2023
P. Doomen, *Introduction to SparxSystems Enterprise Architect*,
https://doi.org/10.1007/978-1-4842-9312-6_2

Case 2-1: Documenting an Enterprise Architecture

I keep six honest serving men (they taught me all I knew); their names are What and Why, When and How, and Where and Who.

—Rudyard Kipling

More than 40 years ago, business consultant John Zachman came up with a framework to describe the architecture of organizations. Despite its age, it still offers a fresh and complete view on enterprises, reaching far beyond the realm of information systems. As such, it is an ideal starting point for any attempt to model the architecture of any organization or enterprise.

Enterprise Architecture and the Zachman Framework

My framework is the application of classification theory to descriptive representations of an object.

—John Zachman

The framework itself is two-dimensional. The first dimension covers the primitive interrogatives why, how, what, who, where, and when – Rudyard Kipling's friends.

The second dimension relates to the philosophical idea of reification transformations: a series of steps from an abstract idea to its implementation. The steps used in the Zachman Framework are identification, definition, representation, specification, configuration, and instantiation. Each of these is related to a perspective. For example, the identification layer is the "planner's view" or the "executive perspective": it defines the business purpose and strategy.

8

As such, the Zachman Framework has 6x6 cells, each of which contains a specific model. For example, the highest-level cell in the "How" column contains a process list, while the level below is a process model. In general, it is a good idea to start with simple lists when creating an enterprise architecture.

Notes on the Use of the Zachman Framework

Like with any framework, there are lots of valid criticisms to be made. For example, it is based on a conceptual argument, not an empirical one. Still, almost all other enterprise architecture frameworks borrow heavily from the Zachman Framework.

No one in their right mind implements all 36 cells to their full detail. In general, it is good practice to limit the effort to the most relevant cells. Don't skip the "Why" column as it is essential to understand the goals of the enterprise, but be careful not to spend energy just to "document the full EA." Especially when time is limited, focus is important.

The Zachman Framework is not a methodology, but rather an ontology. It does not prescribe any process or even roles and responsibilities for documenting an enterprise architecture. This can be seen as a shortcoming, but it is also a benefit: it keeps the framework simple and understandable, without the need for extensive training.

Applying the Zachman Framework in Enterprise Architect

7000 years of history say that architecture is the only way to deal with complexity and change.

—John Zachman

A whitepaper on the Zachman Framework can be found at the SparxSystems website (sparxsystems.com), which discusses its usage and implementation. The MDG technology that accompanies this whitepaper is available in the Ultimate edition of EA, but you can easily apply the main ideas from the Zachman Framework by using the Professional version of EA.

We will loosely use the Zachman Framework, especially the top two or three layers of it: the contextual, conceptual, and logical views. The physical, detailed, and functioning levels would take us too deep and too far, especially for a first version of an Enterprise Architecture model.

Now on to the main concepts of Enterprise Architect. This will help us to structure and visualize the Systemplar Enterprise Architecture.

Repositories, Projects, and the Model Wizard

At first, the EA user interface will be cold and empty. But it won't take us long before we start our first project... But let me first introduce you to two important concepts of Enterprise Architect.

Enterprise Architect presents itself as a user interface that can connect with database repositories. Each database repository, or repository for short, contains the information belonging to one project. So a "project" in the EA user interface shows the information of a certain "repository" that is sitting somewhere: on a local storage such as the hard drive of your laptop, on a database server, or in the cloud, which is basically also a database server.

For small projects such as the Systemplar Enterprise Architecture project, a simple local repository will suffice. If you work with more than say three people on a project, you will want to move to a database server. And if these people want to work remotely, the cloud option is a good idea.

Note   To make things concrete, we will use the case of a company
called "Systemplar." Of course, you can change this name to whatever
project you are working on for your own company or organization.

Let's now start to document the Systemplar Enterprise Architecture:

1. On the EA Start Page, click "Create New…."

2. Create a folder "Systemplar." In that folder, create a
    subfolder "Enterprise Architecture."

3. Create a file "SEAM" (for "Systemplar Enterprise
    Architecture Model"). The file will get the extension "qea."
    This is a Microsoft Access–based database file (Figure 2-1).

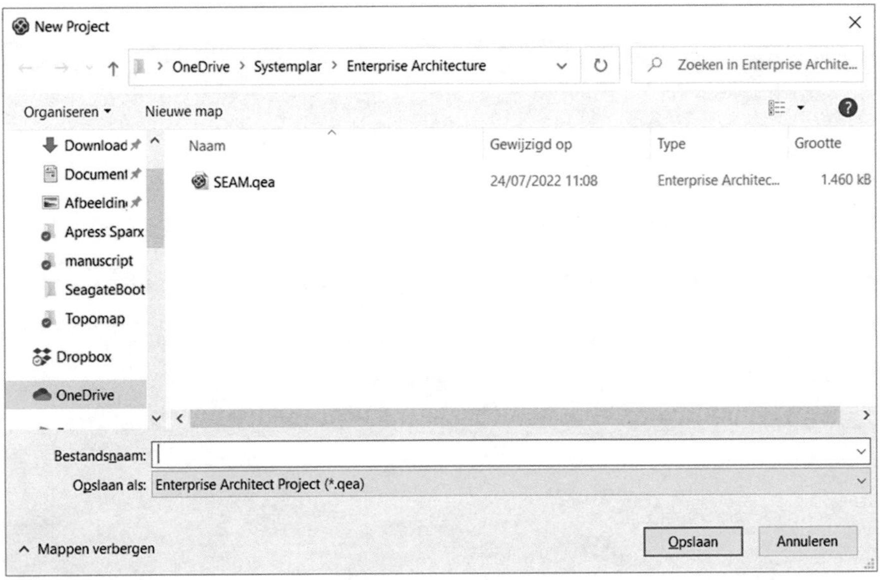

Figure 2-1. *Saving a model in a database file*

We now have an empty model. Time to populate it! One way to do that
is by invoking the Model Wizard (Figure 2-2). Right-click "Model" in the
Project Browser and choose "Add a model using the Model Wizard…."

The user interface will show a list of different models, each with multiple versions like a basic version and more intricate ones. If you find a model that matches your current task, just click "Create model(s)," and it will be added to the current model. Repeat if you need to add other diagrams based on the provided templates.

This is of course a great way to kick-start any project where you have a clear idea on what diagrams to start with. In the following example, the Model Wizard has just created a use case diagram and corresponding Project Browser structure with a folder for the actors and one for the use cases. I suggest you take your time to scroll through the list of available patterns – the list is huge and goes from standard UML type diagrams like class diagrams, deployment diagrams, sequence and activity diagrams over requirements diagrams, strategy maps, road-mapping diagrams, mind maps, and user interface diagrams (Figure 2-3).

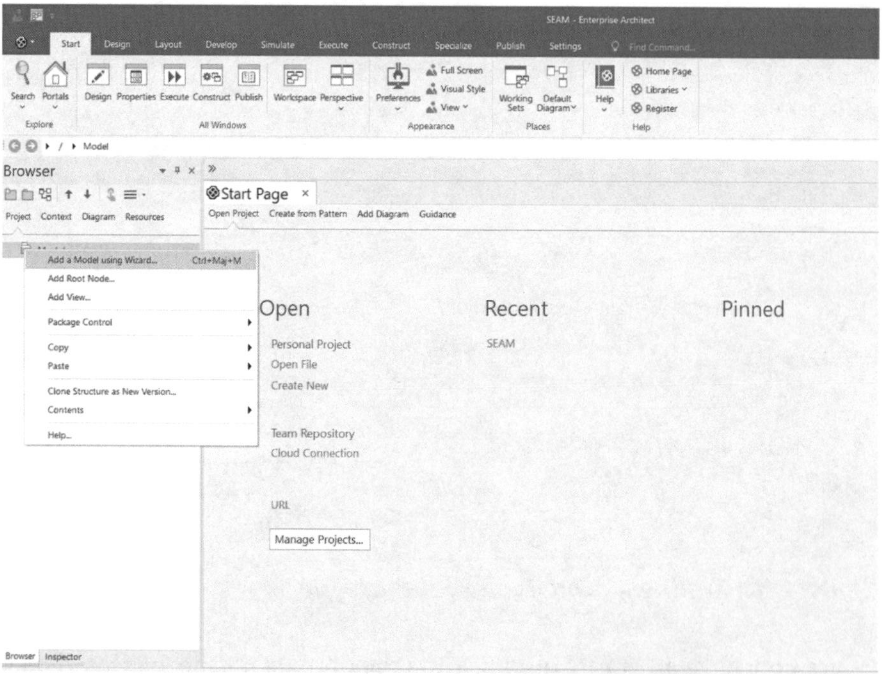

Figure 2-2. *Invoking the Model using Wizard – the Model Wizard*

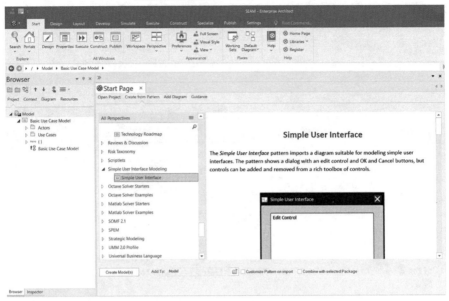

Figure 2-3. *The Model Wizard for user interfaces*

Because we use the Professional version of EA, in which the Zachman
Framework pattern is not included, we will just create a nested package
structure (Figure 2-4) with the help of the Model Wizard. As its name
indicates, this will create a nested package structure, but it also creates a
diagram that simply shows the table of contents of our structure. Easy!

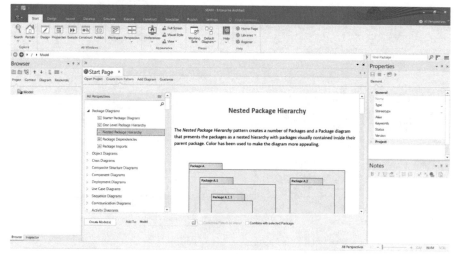

Figure 2-4. *Model wizard – nested package structure*

The Big Five of Enterprise Architect: Models, Elements, Diagrams, Connectors, and Packages

Now before we go any further adding contents to our model, let's first review what I call the "Big Five" of Enterprise Architect: the models, the elements, the packages, the diagrams, and the connectors. Once you know their roles and their relationship, you can start modeling in EA.

Models

We already encountered the concept of a "model": a model is a representation of some aspect of reality. For example, a use case model shows a system, the actors that work on the system, and the functions they use in the system. Any EA project contains one or multiple models, which might show a representation of related aspects of reality. For example, our SEAM project will contain one Enterprise Architecture model with

different submodels, some of them showing data-related diagrams, others
event representations, and still others people-related views such as a role-
based security model. Let us keep things simple and assume that a project
contains exactly one model.

Elements and Diagrams

Any model contains diagrams, elements, and connectors. A diagram is
just a visual way to show elements and connectors. Elements are typically
representations of a concept that is a part of reality. In our use case
diagram, the system is represented by a big rectangle, containing ovals that
represent use cases. Stick figures represent actors, which are drawn outside
of the system rectangle.

In Enterprise Architect, elements live their own life, separate from the
diagrams that show them. So, an element can exist without any diagram
containing it. It can even show up in multiple diagrams, yet exist only once.

This is a crucial feature of modeling tools such as EA. When creating
diagrams in tools such as Microsoft Visio, an element only exists by virtue
of the diagram that shows it. When the diagram is deleted, the element
ceases to exist. In Visio, any element can only exist once.

If you think about it, the fact that EA allows you to separate elements
from diagrams is no coincidence. On the contrary, it is the reason that you
want to use a modeling tool for complex models like the SEAM:

- Change and forget: When you change a property of an
  element, every diagram that shows it will be adapted
  to the new reality. Suppose you modeled a system like
  "CRM" and used it on four or more diagrams already
  (you might even have lost count!). Later on, you learn
  that they use the Zoho CRM system. Now you just look
  up "CRM" in the Project Browser or on any diagram,
  change the name to "Zoho CRM," and voila, each and
  every diagram will show the new name.

- Use multiple times: Instead of recreating the "CRM" system every time you need it on a diagram, you just drag it from the Project Browser. This saves time and effort and guarantees the consistency of your model.

- Delete diagrams, keep the elements: A diagram is just a way to show elements and their connections. You might experiment with diagrams to show a certain part of reality, but end up understanding that 50% of these representations are not adequate for the intended audience. No worries: you can safely delete the diagram while keeping the essential information in the model.

Let's try these three actions in Enterprise Architect:

1. **Create a new diagram**

   In the Project Browser, right-click the "Model" root (a top-level package is called a "root" in Enterprise Architect) and choose "Add a View" (a package directly below a "root" is called a "View" in Enterprise Architect). Then simply add packages as needed to the newly created view by right-clicking the view and choosing "Add a Package."

   Still in the Project Browser, right-click Package A (this is just an example, we will give the packages more meaningful names later). Choose "Add diagram..." ➤ "Component" ➤ "UML:Simple Component" (Figure 2-5).

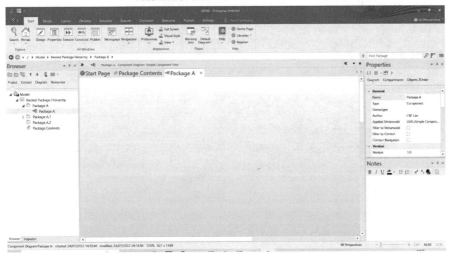

Figure 2-5. *Creating a diagram*

2. **Add an element "CRM" to it**

Right-click the diagram and choose "Insert – Show
Toolbox." The toolbox "Simple Component"
appears. From this toolbox, drag the "component"
element to the diagram. A component is created –
change its name to "CRM" (Figure 2-6).

Remark that the Project Browser now shows an
element "Component1" that gets renamed to
"CRM" as soon as you confirm the renaming by
pressing enter.

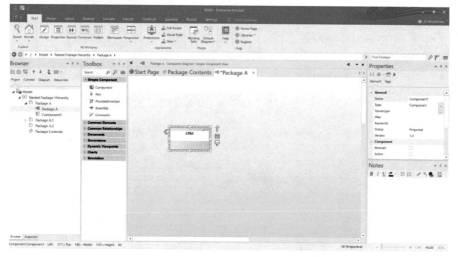

Figure 2-6. *Adding the CRM element to a diagram*

3. **Create a second diagram**

   In the Project Browser, right-click a package and
   choose "Add Diagram." Give the diagram the
   name "Diagram 2." It does not have to be in the
   same package as the original diagram, but it can
   (Figure 2-7).

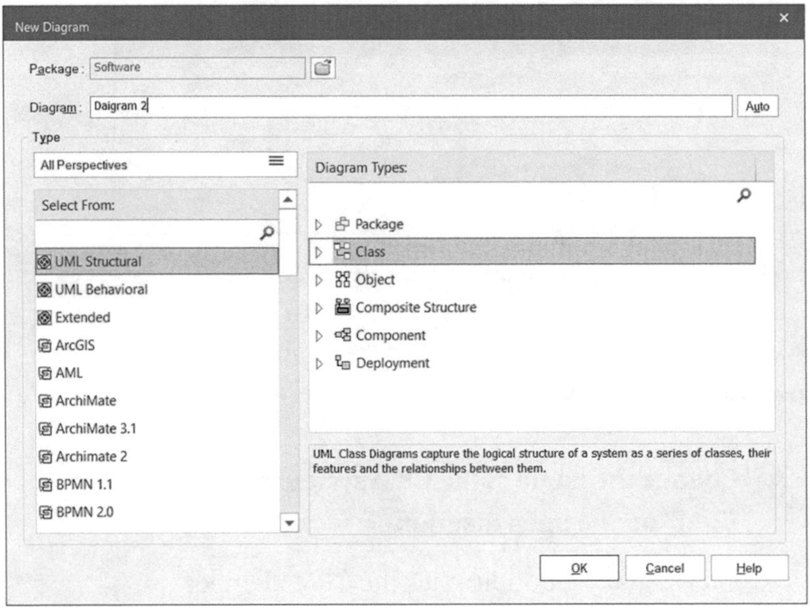

Figure 2-7. *Adding a second diagram*

4. **Add the "CRM" element to it from the Project Browser**

   Drag the CRM element from the Project Browser to the diagram "Diagram 2." A pop-up shows "Paste CRM" (Figure 2-8). Check the checkbox "Only show if Ctrl pressed" to indicate that inserting existing elements to diagrams as a link should be the default behavior.

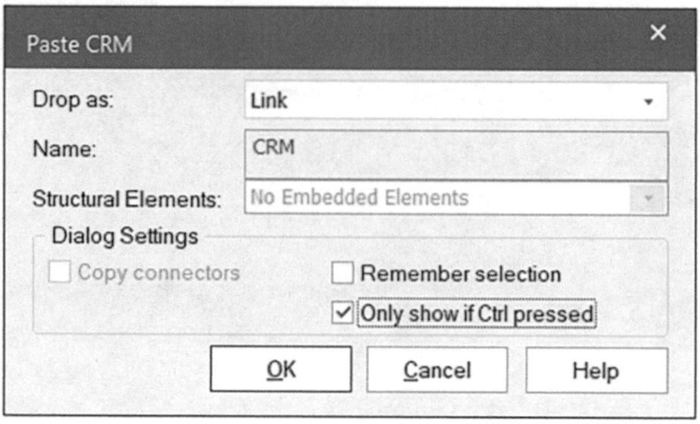

Figure 2-8. *Paste CRM*

5. **Change the name of the CRM system to "Zoho
   CRM" on the open diagram**

   On Diagram 2, double-click the CRM element.
   The dialog window with the properties of the CRM
   element shows. Change its name to "Zoho CRM"
   and confirm by clicking OK (Figure 2-9).

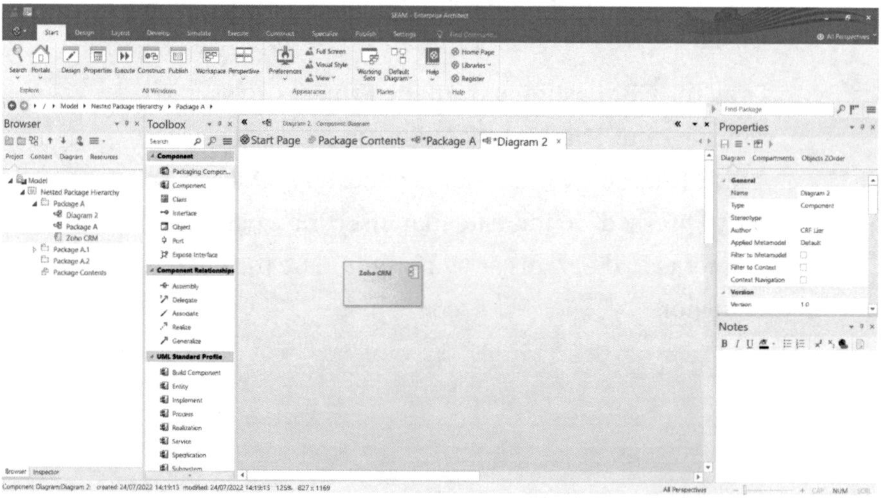

Figure 2-9. *Changing the name of the CRM element to "Zoho CRM"*

6. **Verify that the name has been changed in the Project Browser and on the original diagram as well**

   Now you already see that the element's name has been changed in the Project Browser. Open the original diagram either by double-clicking it in the Project Browser or by clicking its tab at the top of the central window (Figure 2-10).

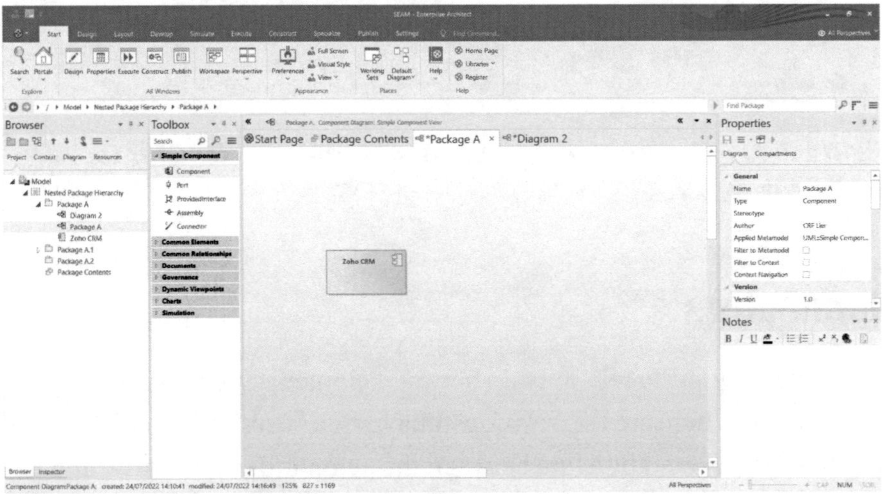

Figure 2-10. *Verifying the name has changed on both diagrams*

7. **Delete the diagram and verify that the element still exists**

   Now delete the diagram by right-clicking it in the Project Browser and choosing "Delete Package A." The element "CRM" still sits in the Project Browser. Even if you delete the second diagram, it keeps on living (Figure 2-11). You have to delete it from the Project Browser if you really want it to be gone.

21

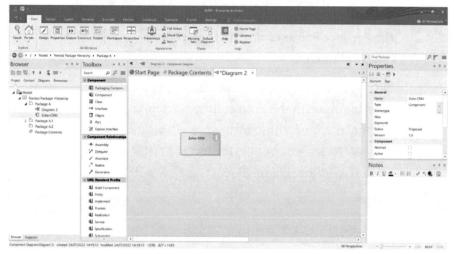

Figure 2-11. *Deleting a diagram doesn't cause its elements to
disappear*

Connectors

Connectors show the relationship between elements. In the simple use
case diagram, there are two relationship types: a "uses" relationship,
which is represented by a line between the actor and the use case, and a
"contains" relationship, which is implicit – the use cases are drawn inside
the rectangle of the system that contains the use case.

Like with elements, connectors have a bit of a life of their own. You
can't see them in the Project Browser, but they are there. If two elements
are connected with each other via a connector, and you drag both of the
elements to a new diagram, the link will show up.

Note   There are a few exceptions to this rule, but for now, let's
assume this is always the case.

How does this work in Enterprise Architect?

1. **Create a second system**

   Drag a component from the Toolbox to the diagram and call it "Document Archive."

2. **Create a connection**

   Click the Zoho CRM system on the diagram. At the top-right corner, an arrow appears. Drag this arrow to the middle of the Document Archive.

   As soon as you release the mouse button, a menu shows up. Choose "usage" to indicate that the Zoho CRM system uses the Document Archive (Figure 2-12).

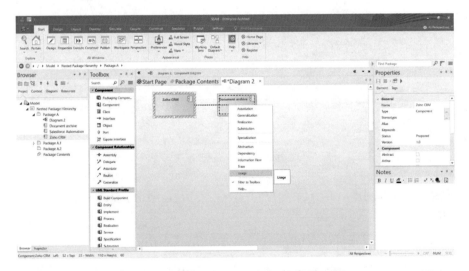

Figure 2-12. *Creating a connection between elements*

3. **Create a second diagram and add both systems to it**

Now create a second diagram and add first the Zoho CRM system to it by dragging it from the Project Browser. Repeat for the Document Archive (Figure 2-13).

As you can see, the diagrams can each have their own layout yet still show the same information: that there is a "use" link between the Zoho CRM and the Document Archive.

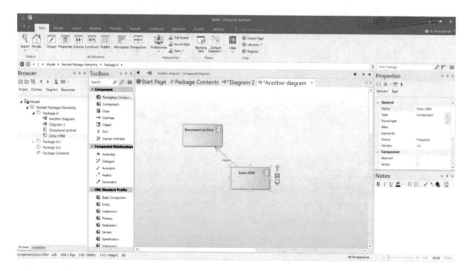

Figure 2-13. *Add both elements to a new diagram and see the connection showing up*

Delete the Connection Between Both Elements

As a last step, what if you discover that the link between the Zoho CRM and the Document Archive doesn't actually exist? Can you delete it? Of course. Just select the connector on the diagram, right-click, and choose "Delete connector."

A dialog window pops up (Figure 2-14), asking if you want to actually delete the connector or that you merely want to hide it. Select "Delete" and check "Don't show this again" to make this the default behavior. If you want to undo this setting, go to the Ribbon: "Start" ➤ "Preferences" ➤ "Preferences" ➤ "Links" and check the box "Prompt on Connector Deletes."

Figure 2-14. *Remove Connector*

Packages

The last element of the "Big Five" is packages, which is just a way to organize the contents of the Project Browser. They work more or less like the folder structure of a file system. So in essence they can be nested, and they can contain an unlimited amount of diagrams and elements.

Two levels of packages are a bit special:

- Root node: The topmost level of the package hierarchy consists of root nodes.

- Views: The level just below the root node.

In former versions of EA, there were some limitations to what you could do with root nodes and views (such as you could not move elements between views or root nodes), but luckily, these limitations have been eliminated. The only limitation that is left is that you cannot create or move diagrams and elements directly under the root node.

Wrapping It All Up

To wrap this up before we start with the real Systemplar Enterprise Architecture Model (SEAM), we keep in mind

- An EA project is a repository that corresponds to a database where all information about the project is kept. The project is structured with the help of packages. The topmost level is called the root, of which there can be more than one, and the second level is called the view.

- Diagrams and elements find their place under a view or under a package that is part of another package. You cannot add diagrams or elements directly under a root.

- A model is the whole of the diagrams, elements, and connectors corresponding to the project.

- A diagram is part of a project (or model) and can show zero, one, or more elements. If it shows elements, by default it also shows their connectors if they exist.

- An element is a typed entity that belongs to the project. When showing on a diagram, it gets a visual representation that can change and that can differ from one diagram to another.

- A connector is a relationship between two elements, which can be the same. Connectors by default show on diagrams, although they can be hidden.

Creating a Strategy Map in EA

A Strategy Map is a representation of the topmost cell in the "Why" column of the Zachman Framework. The Strategy Map in Figure 2-15 shows

- The mission and the vision of the company: The "reason it exists" (top products/services at an affordable price) and the "big plan for the future" (become the world market leader in seven years' time). This looks clear enough for now.

- The (intangible) assets of the company: Its partner network and its reseller and service network. Still to be clarified: Are these one, overlapping, or separate networks?

- The initiatives that are being taken to improve the assets: Each of these might become a set of projects later on. To be clarified.

- The relations between the mission, vision, assets, and initiatives.

In a later phase, you could opt for additional elements such as objectives, perspectives, and other information.

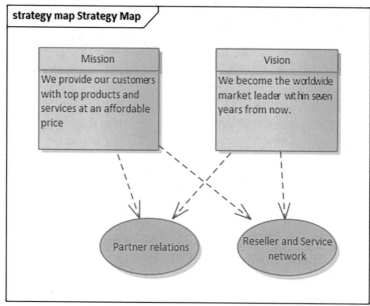

Figure 2-15.   *The Strategy Map*

Let's create this simple Strategy Map step by step:

1. **Rename "Package A" and "Package A.1"**

    Right-click "Package A" in the Project Browser
    and select "Properties" ➤ "Properties." In the
    dialog window that shows, rename the package to
    "Motivation" (Figure 2-16). Do the same for the
    underlying package "Package A.1" and rename it to
    "Strategy."

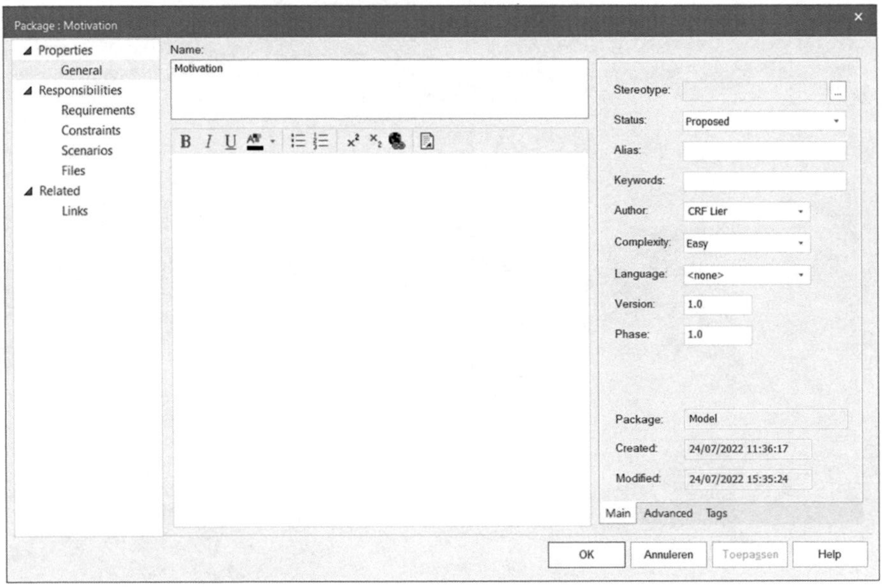

Figure 2-16. *Renaming the package to "Motivation"*

2. **Add a diagram of type "Strategy Map"**

   Right-click the "Strategy" package and choose "Add diagram…." Pick the "Strategy Map" type from the list.

   A toolbox appears (Figure 2-17) that contains all the element types relevant to strategy maps. There is even a section with Patterns that you can use if you want to create a more formal Strategy Map.

Figure 2-17. *The toolbox for creating strategy maps*

For now, we will loosely use the element types
to model what we have found in the Systemplar
Strategy Presentation.

3. **Create the elements for "Mission" and "Vision"**

   Drag an element of type "Mission" from the Toolbox
   to the diagram and call it "Mission" (Figure 2-18).
   Double-click it and add the description. Do the
   same for the "Vision" element.

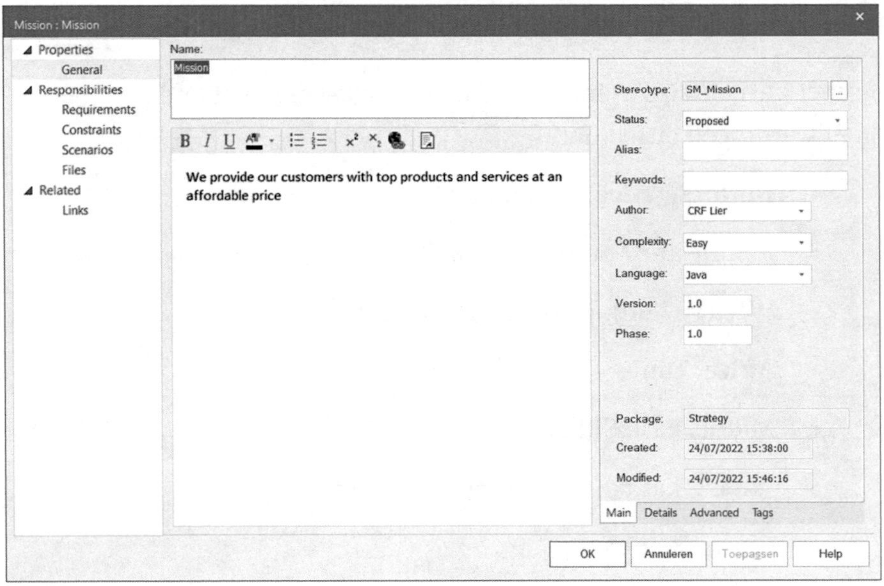

Figure 2-18. *Creating a "mission" element*

4. **Create the elements for the "intangible assets" and relate them to the "mission" and "vision"**

   Create two intangible assets "Partner relations" and "Reseller and Service network." Select the "Mission" element and use the Quicklinker (arrow at the top right) to add a dependency on the "Mission" element to the "Partner relations" element. Do the same for the other relations.

5. **Create the "Initiative" elements and relate them to the assets**

   Finally, let's add three strategic initiatives and relate them to the correct asset. The result is a first version of the Strategy Map. We already have something to show and discuss!

The List of Geographic Locations

Another file contains a simple text file with a list of the different offices,
roughly arranged by region:

- North America: Pittsburgh

- Middle and South America: San Salvador

- Western Europe: Reims (Headquarters)

- Africa: Tunis

- Middle East: Shiraz

- Russia, Kazakhstan, Mongolia: Moscow

- China: Xiamen

- India: Kochi

- Japan: Kobe

- Australia, New Zealand: Sydney

There's surely more structure to this than just a list of regions with the
name of the city where the local office is, so for now, just put the list of
locations in EA as shown in Figure 2-19.

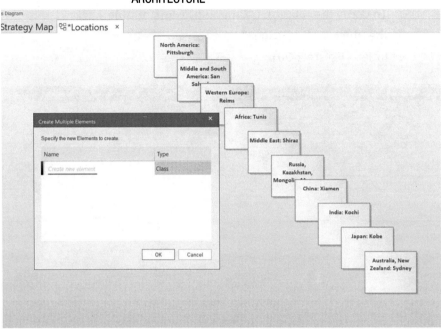

Figure 2-19. *Adding the locations to a diagram*

1. Via the Ribbon "Design" ➤ "Element" ➤ "Add
   Element" ➤ "Multiple elements," paste the elements
   from the list, one by one (Figure 2-19).

2. Since there isn't a "type" for "location," just add them
   as "classes." Now the diagram shows the locations.

3. Now drag the objective "Strengthen presence in
   the Middle East" to the locations diagram, and add
   a connection of type "association" to the location
   element "Middle East: Shiraz."

4. Then delete the objective element from the diagram.
   This way, the connection between the elements will
   not be lost when more information gets added to
   the model.

5.   To verify the relation is indeed present, double-click
the object "Middle East" and consult "Related –
links" (Figure 2-20).

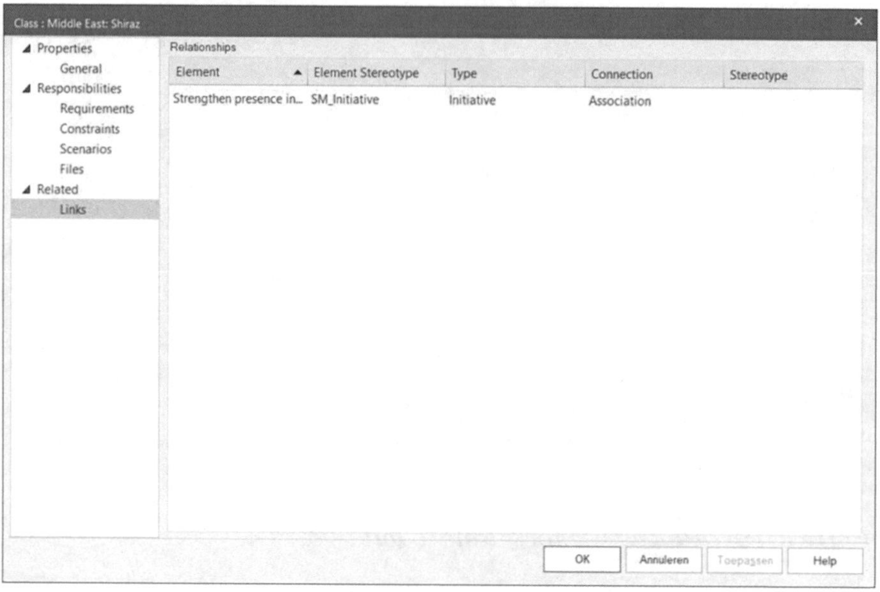

Figure 2-20.   *The relationship from the "Initiative" to the location
"Middle East" is still there as you can see in the element properties*

Summary

In this chapter, we have covered the essentials of every Enterprise Architect
model. We saw how to create packages and diagrams and how to add
elements to these. We discovered that elements can exist in the model
even if they are not present on any diagram. Furthermore, we added
connections between elements and saw that these by default will show up
on any diagram where these elements are added.

There's still a long way to go, so you'll need to get more details about
the projects that are going on at Systemplar, an overview of the processes
that are crucial to the business. You'll learn about this in the next chapter.

CHAPTER 3

Working with Elements

Elements are the building blocks of any Enterprise Architect model. It is tempting to compare them to the shapes you use in drawing tools like Visio or PowerPoint. To a certain extent, the comparison holds: you can "draw" them in a similar way as you draw a rectangle or any other shape in a drawing tool. You can then move them around on the diagram, change their properties such as color or border width, enlarge or shrink them... In this chapter, you'll see how easy it is to work with elements in the EA model.

Elements

Elements are more than just a shape. This becomes clear when you delete them from a diagram. Although they are removed from the diagram, an element isn't actually deleted, as it still appears in the Project Browser. The following steps show how easy it is to check:

1. Open the "Strategy Map" in the "Motivation" view of the SEAM. It contains seven elements (Figure 3-1). Select one of these, for example, the "Vision" element, by clicking it.

© Peter Doomen 2023
P. Doomen, *Introduction to SparxSystems Enterprise Architect*,
https://doi.org/10.1007/978-1-4842-9312-6_3

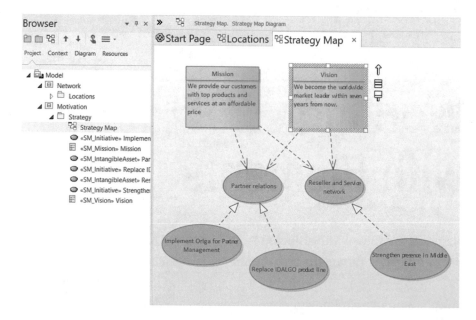

Figure 3-1. *Selecting an element on a diagram*

2. Delete the element from the diagram by pressing the "delete" key on your keyboard. The element "Vision" is gone (Figure 3-2)!

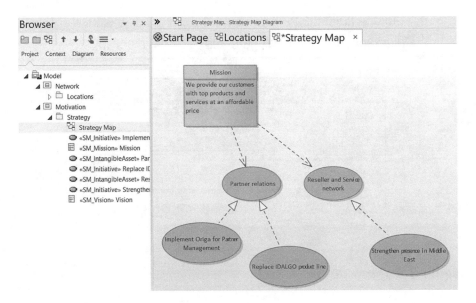

Figure 3-2. *Deleting an element from the diagram*

3. Verify the element still exists in the Project Browser. "<<SM_Vision>>" Vision still shows up, so it hasn't been deleted, it was just removed from the diagram.

4. Add it back to the diagram. Drag the "Vision" element to the diagram. It reappears, and even all connectors are still intact.

Note   The first time you do this, a dialog box (Figure 3-3) shows up asking what you want to do. Do you want to drop "Vision" as a…

- Link: No copy will be created; the original element is used.

- Instance: The "Vision" element will be copied, and the copy is added to the diagram.

- Child: A child element will be created to the "Vision" element, and that child gets added to the diagram.

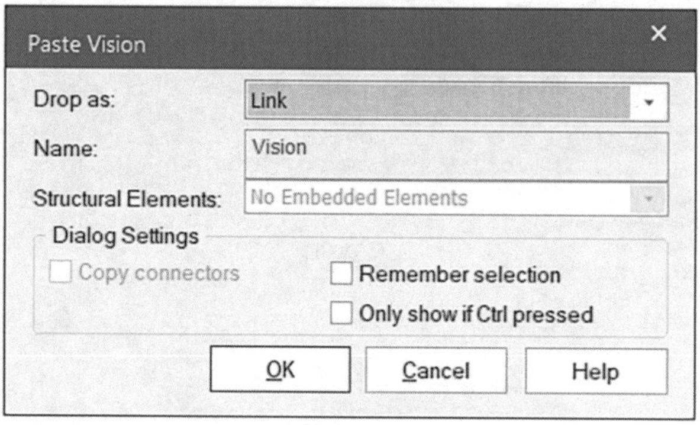

Paste Vision

Drop as:	Link
Name:	Vision
Structural Elements:	No Embedded Elements

Dialog Settings

☐ Copy connectors   ☐ Remember selection
                      ☐ Only show if Ctrl pressed

[OK]   [Cancel]   [Help]

Figure 3-3. *Paste vision*

Creating copies of elements is bad modeling practice. Only very specific circumstances justify creating a copy, and these are rare. Therefore, I suggest you check the boxes "Remember selection" and "Only show if Ctrl is pressed." This way, adding elements without making copies that clutter your model becomes the standard.

Because you can add any element from the Project Browser to a diagram, you can reuse existing information so you don't have to copy elements.

Elements Can Appear on Zero, One, or More Diagrams

The fact that you can add an element from the Project Browser to a diagram without copying it also means that elements can appear on more than one diagram. You just look up the element in the Project Browser and drag it to the diagram. We already touched on that in the previous chapter.

You could say that elements have a life of their own: they exist in the model, irrespective of their use on diagrams. This is a big difference with drawing tools such as Visio: here, a shape only exists if it is shown somewhere, and you cannot have multiple representations of the same thing on different diagrams. If you need to have the "Vision" element on more than one diagram in a drawing tool, you have to create a copy. Now each time the element changes, you have to maintain all copies of it. This quickly becomes cumbersome as the model grows.

So the decoupling of elements and diagrams is not a bug, but a feature of Enterprise Architect. It is a real time saver, and it also avoids confusion because there is only one version of the truth.

Elements and Their Extended Properties

Besides the fact that elements have a life of their own separate from diagrams, there is a second big difference between the shapes of a drawing tool and elements in Enterprise Architect. Elements have properties that you can customize. Let's explore a few of these properties.

In the Strategy Map, double-click the "Vision" element. A dialog box pops up that shows the properties of the "Vision" element (Figure 3-4) such as the name, the description, the status, and a ton more.

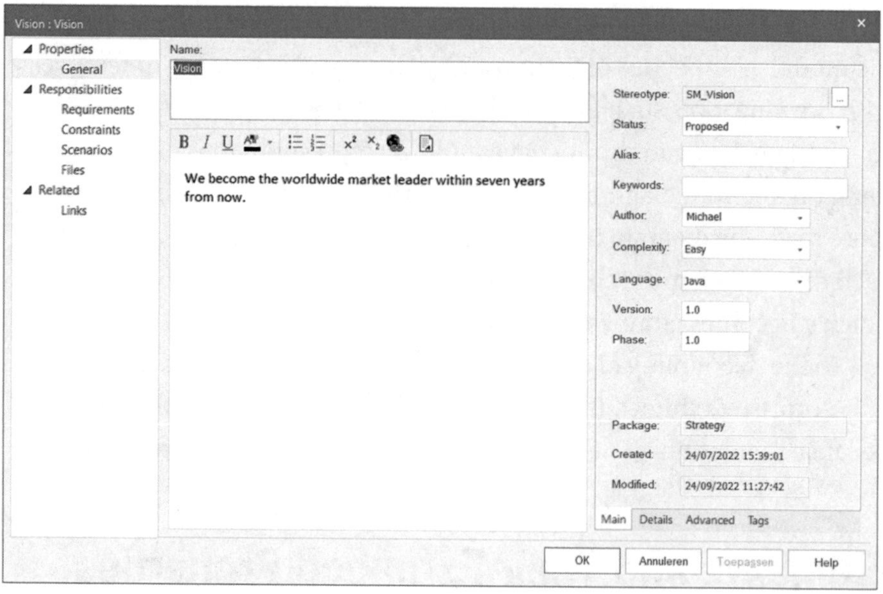

Figure 3-4. *Properties of the vision element*

General Properties

General properties – General include

- Name: The name of the element. It is not mandatory to have unique names for elements, but it is advisable to do so. If you change the name, it will change on all diagrams where the element is shown.

- Description: A more extensive description of the element in the form of a Rich Text Format (RTF) file. So you can use formatting (bold, italics, lists, color, etc.) and even links. The rightmost icon allows you to create a "linked document" which is also an RTF file. See the next section for more information on linked documents.

- Stereotype: The "kind" of element. Stereotypes influence how an element looks. For example, when you create an element, its default appearance (size, color, etc.) depends on the stereotype. More on stereotypes in Chapter 8.

- Status: This is useful when you review the model. Elements start their life in the "Proposed" status, then go to "Validated," "Approved," and eventually "Implemented," if that is applicable.

- Alias: An alternative name for the element. There is a neat trick to use this on diagrams. More on that in Chapter 5.

- Keywords: Add some keywords that can be used for filtering. Also, this field is useful in combination with diagrams. See Chapter 5.

- Author: The name of the user that created the element. Can be changed.

- Complexity: Useful for certain element types like requirements, use cases, classes, processes, etc.

- Language: Applies to "implementation" type elements. Less useful for our SEAM.

- Version: A number (or actually a string) indicating the version of the element. In combination with diagram filtering, this provides a simple but elegant way to show a changing architecture. See Chapter 5.

- Phase: Similar to Version.

Under the "Details" tab, there are properties that relate to typical UML class models. These are less important for our purposes. Also, the "Advanced" tab contains specialized stuff that we don't need for our SEAM.

The last tab, called "Tags," allows us to store custom properties that will help us to extend the information modeling capabilities of Enterprise Architect considerably. We will talk about tags in Chapter 8.

Besides that, there are some read-only properties that show the element's package, created and modified date.

Linked Documents

Any element in Enterprise Architect can have a linked document. These linked documents are RTF files and are stored in the Enterprise Architect repository itself. You can create a linked document by right-clicking the element and choosing "Linked Document" or by selecting the element and using the shortcut "Ctrl+Alt+D."

When you create a linked document, there is an option to base the linked document on a template. For example, for the "Vision" element, it would make sense to choose "Mission/Vision" as a template (Figure 3-5).

Figure 3-5. *Linked document*

This is a great way to standardize documentation in any Enterprise Architect model. More on document generation in Chapter 7.

While it is easy to create a linked document, it is less obvious how to delete a linked document (Figure 3-6).

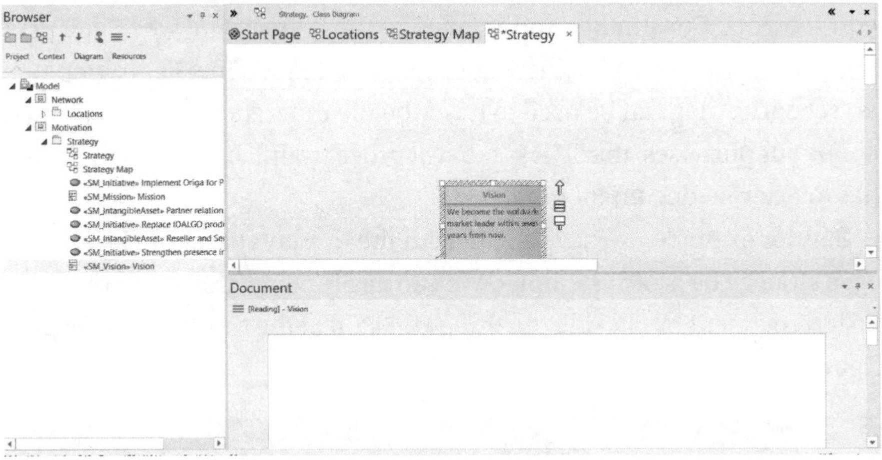

Figure 3-6.   *Delete linked document*

To delete a linked document

- Right-click the element in the Project Browser or on a diagram.

- Select "Properties" ➤ "Linked document."

- A separate window containing the linked document appears underneath the diagram.

- Click the icon with the three horizontal lines at the top left of the linked document window.

- Choose "Delete linked document" from the context menu and confirm.

Responsibilities and Files

The "Properties" window has multiple tabs, which you can find on the left-hand side of the window.

Under the "Responsibilities" tab, you will find still other properties like Requirements, Constraints, and Scenarios: these are useful when you use Enterprise Architect for business and functional modeling. For example, the "scenarios" tag can be used to describe the different paths of a use case.

For our purposes, the "Files" tab will prove useful: here, you can create links to external documentation.

Say, for example, we have a PDF with the presentation from last year's strategy days of Systemplar. We can easily attach this file to the "Vision" element by clicking the three-dot icon at the top of the Links tab (Figure 3-7).

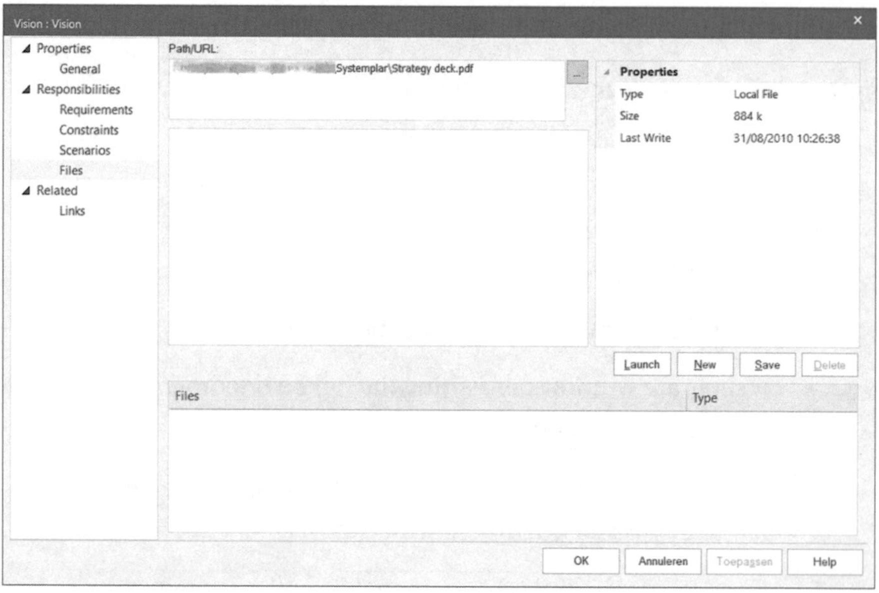

Figure 3-7. *Link Files*

Then just choose the file and confirm by clicking "Save." The file then appears in the file list at the bottom.

To open the file, select the filename and click "Launch."

Note: To prevent link rot, it is a good idea to create one separate folder to store all linked documents, unless there is a good reason not to do so (e.g., confidentiality).

Related Elements

The section "Related" shows all elements that are related to the current one (Figure 3-8).

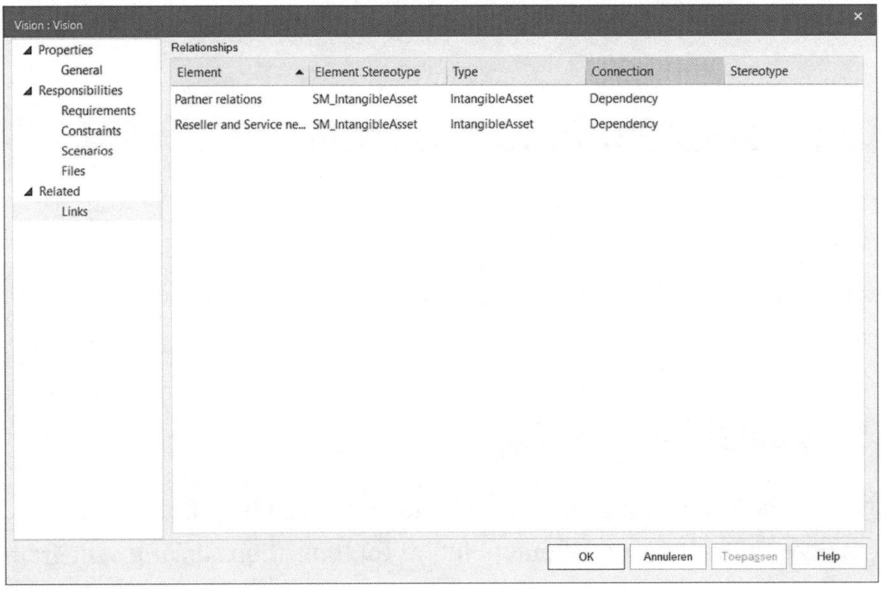

Figure 3-8. *Related elements*

Not only does it show the relationships, you can even act on the relationships. Right-click any relation and a pop-up shows:

- Hide relation: Hide the relation in the current diagram.

- Relationship properties: Like elements, relationships have properties. More on that in Chapter 4.

- Locate related element: Put the focus on the related element in the Project Browser.

- Delete relationship: Delete the relationship from the model. This is different from option 1 "Hide relation": the relationship is actually deleted, not merely made invisible.

Adding Elements to the Model

In Chapter 2, we already saw how you can add elements to a model relatively quickly. Yet there is a method that is even faster, another one that is more visual, and a third one that is very flexible. Let's consider these one by one.

The Visual Way

The most common method to add elements to a model is by clicking the stereotype of the required element in the Toolbox, then clicking a diagram to create the element. In fact, this is how we built the Strategy Map in Chapter 2.

If the Toolbox is not visible, activate it via "Design" ➤ "Toolbox." Once the toolbox is visible, it will show the most commonly used sets of stereotypes. You can activate other sets by clicking the icon with the three horizontal lines at the top right of the toolbox, then selecting the appropriate set.

This is a very visual but also very slow method, especially when you have lots of elements to add. There are two ways to speed this up:

- Method 1: Use the Quicklinker. Select an element. At its top, a white arrow appears (Figure 3-9). Drag this to an empty space on the diagram and release; then select the element and the relation to create. For example, if we want to create a location (stereotype: class) connected to the Pittsburgh location, we choose "Class" ➤ "Association." Fill out the name of the new location in the dialog window that appears, and we have not only created the new location but also a relationship.

- Method 2: Use the shortcut Ctrl+click on an empty space on the diagram, which creates an element of the same stereotype as the last one created.

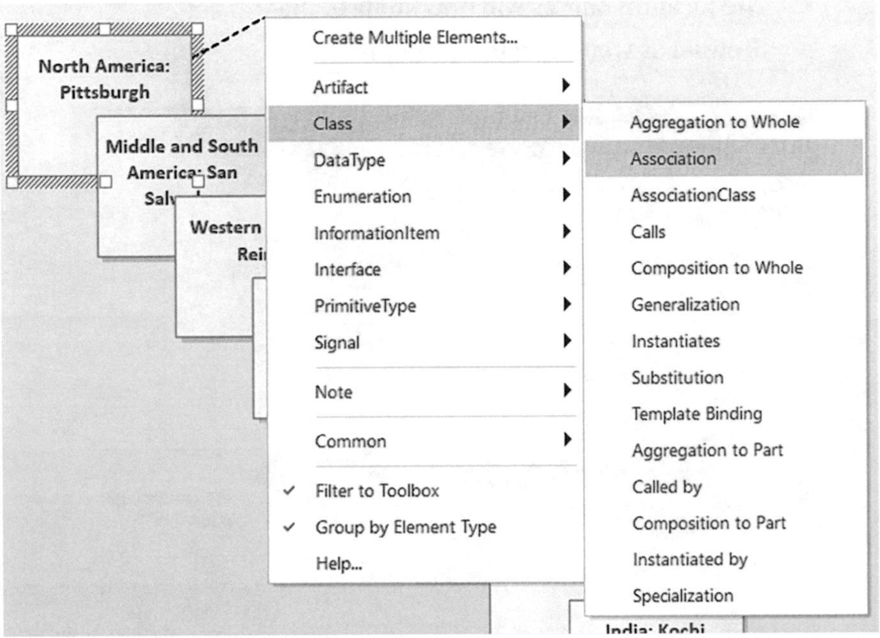

Figure 3-9. *The Quicklinker in action*

The Fastest Way

Suppose we didn't already have the list of locations in our SEAM, but we got a text file with this list.

It is easy to quickly add these to the model with their correct stereotype ("class"):

- Copy the locations list to the clipboard (one line per item).

- In the Ribbon, click "Design" ➤ "Add Element" ➤ "Add Multiple Elements."

- In the dialog window "Create Multiple Elements" (Figure 3-10), right-click "Create new element" and choose "Import Names from Clipboard" and confirm with OK.

- The location names will now show in the Project Browser as well as on the diagram.

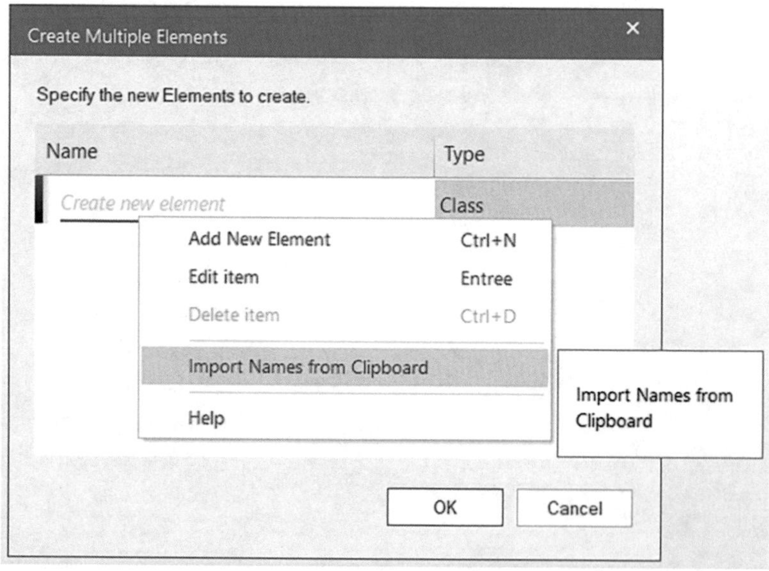

Figure 3-10. *Import names from clipboard*

This is obviously the fastest way to add a bunch of elements to an Enterprise Architect model, provided they are all of the same type and you only need to import names. What if you also want to import their type or other properties such as the description ("notes")?

Flexibility Required? Try the csv Import!

Using the csv import is a bit more complicated than simply importing the names list from the clipboard. There are two steps to take:

1. Make an import specification: Basically, this is a template that specifies what information will be present in the file to import.

2. Do the actual import: Use the import specification to transform the file from an external source to the Enterprise Architect model. You might need to modify this external file in a spreadsheet application before the import succeeds. For example, you have to specify a "type" for each element to create, and you probably want to specify a stereotype as well.

Let's use the process list in a concrete example.

Case 3-1: Importing a Project List into the Enterprise Architecture

We have a spreadsheet (Figure 3-11) with a list of Systemplar business processes and their description. We will convert this to the right format so we can then import this in Enterprise Architect.

	A	B	C	D	E	F	G	H	I
1	Process	Description							
2	Asset management	controlling and planning the operation, maintenance, renewal and disposition of assets, streamlining asset management
3	Business process improvement	measuring efficiency, improve efficiency
4	Customer service	onboarding new customers, service existing customers, customer feedback and complaints management
5	Delivery management process	automatic dispatch, vehicle tracking, delivery planning
6	Finance process	budgeting, financial strategy, financial operations, facilities strategy, facilities operations, financial auditing
7	Human resource process	hiring employees, talent management, benefits management, time and attendance, payroll
8	Marketing process	upstream marketing, downstream marketing, portfolio management, customer relationships management
9	Procurement process	selecting vendors, establish payment terms, negotiation, purchase supplies
10	Product development	idea generation, concept development, market research, launching products, product lifecycle management
11	Project management	starting and executing projects, organising projects in programs and portfolios
12	Sales process	cold sales, upselling, sales automation, streamline quotes and proposals, manage orders and delivery, billing

Figure 3-11. *The process list in a spreadsheet*

This is how we need to change the spreadsheet a bit to successfully import it in Enterprise Architect:

1. Add a column "Type" which is filled with "Activity," since a "process" in Enterprise Architect has "Activity" as the base class.

2. Also, add a column "Stereotype," filled with "process," so the processes would show up correctly in Enterprise Architect.

3. Finally, save the spreadsheet as a csv file.

Next, it's time to turn to Enterprise Architect, where we add a View under the "Model" root called "Function." Under that view, we add a package called "Process list" with a diagram "Process list."

Then, we prepare an import specification. In the Ribbon, we click "Publish" ➤ "CSV" ➤ "Import/Export Specification" (Figure 3-12).

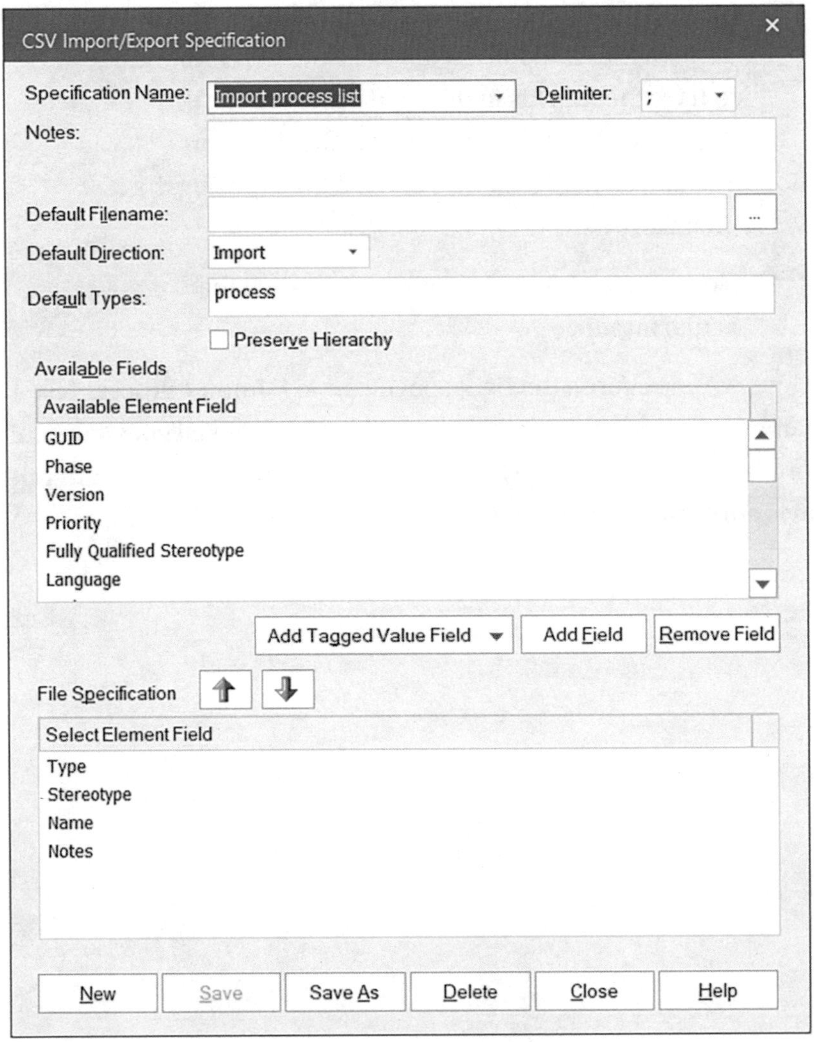

Figure 3-12. *CSV import/export specification*

In the Import/Export Specification dialog, we take these steps:

1. Specify a name ("import process list").

2. Choose a field delimiter and a default direction ("import").

3. Choose four Element Fields by double-clicking them in the Available Fields list. Note: It is important to have these fields in the right order, that is, the column order of the spreadsheet file to import. You can change the order of the fields by using the green arrows.

4. Now it's time for the last and easiest step: the actual import.

Here, we just choose the right specification ("Import Process List") and filename ("process list.csv"). Then we click "Run" and all goes smoothly (Figure 3-13). Apart from the first line (the header with the column titles), all lines are correctly imported in the SEAM.

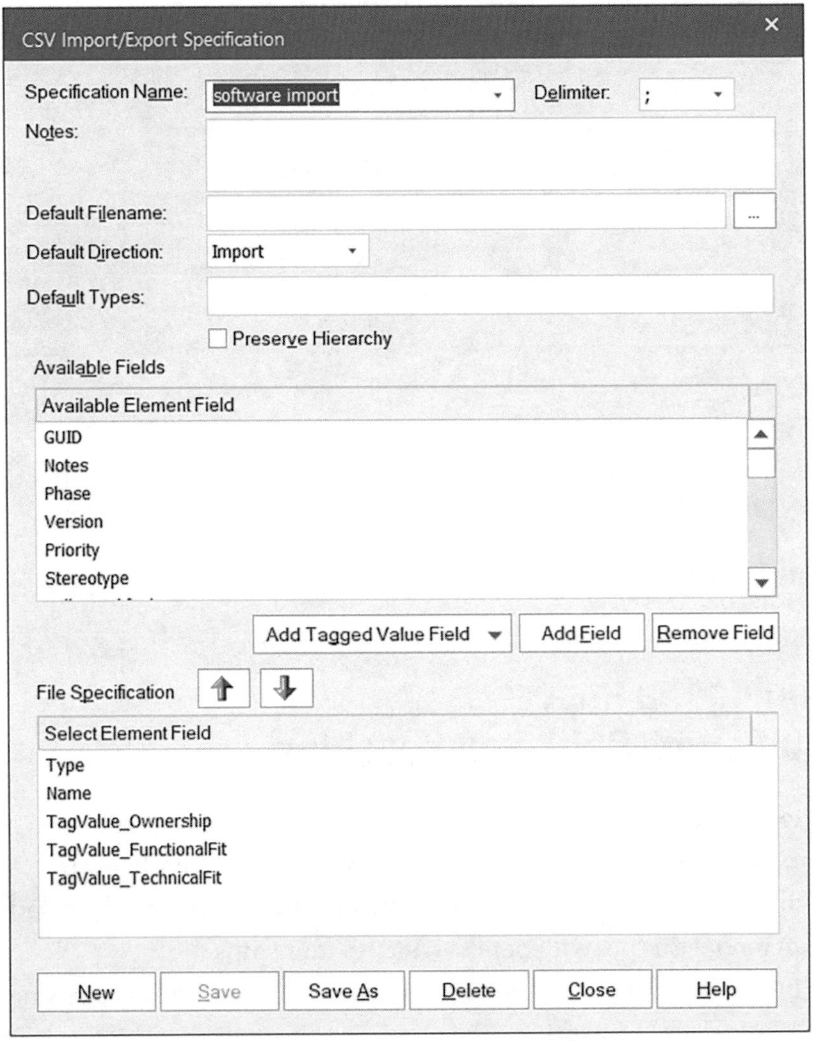

Figure 3-13. *Csv import*

The processes are not added to the diagram, however, so we just select them in the Project Browser and drag them to the process list diagram. With a bit of manual layouting, we finally get a diagram like Figure 3-14.

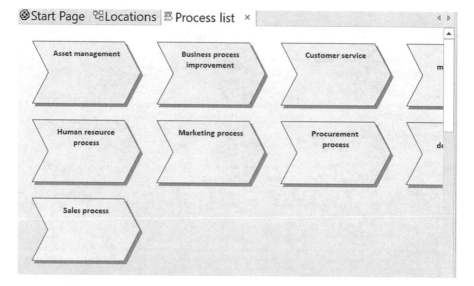

Figure 3-14. *Business process list*

Refining the Import with Parent-Child Relationships

This looks like a very basic list indeed. We can be fairly sure this is incomplete, but let's work with it and see where we get. Probably the descriptions of the processes are actually processes themselves, so perhaps we can model this out with parent-child relationships.

"Business process improvement" would be the umbrella, consisting of two processes "Measuring efficiency" and "Improving efficiency." Likewise, "Customer Service" would become the parent of the processes "Onboarding New Customers," "Service Existing Customers," and so on.

Even if this was only an incomplete list of processes, we should remember the words of John Zachman: "If you put more than one thing in a diagram, you can't see the whole enterprise." No doubt Zachman was right: if the process list would grow to 50 or more processes, just having these on a diagram would already be hard to understand.

So we need a bit of time to restructure the model to reflect this insight that the "processes" are actually an umbrella for the real process list.

First, we refine the process spreadsheet:

1. We add lines for each of the processes under their "umbrella" process.

2. We fill in the "Type" and "Stereotype" for these processes: "Activity" and "Process," respectively.

3. Then we add two columns: CSV_KEY and CSV_PARENT_KEY as the last columns of the spreadsheet.

4. We give each of the umbrella processes a name: P1, P2, and so on. These are filled in in the CSV_KEY column.

5. We also give each of the "child" processes a consecutive number: P1.1, P1.2, and so on, to reflect their relationship with the "parent" process.

6. Finally, we fill in the keys of the parent in the CSV_PARENT_KEY column: P1 for business processes P1.1 and P1.2 and so on.

The file now looks like Figure 3-15.

	A	B	C	D	E	F	G
1	Type	Stereotype	Process	Description	CSV_KEY	CSV_PARENT_KEY	
2	Activity	Process	Asset management	controlling and planning the operation, maintenance	P1		
3	Activity	Process	Controlling and planning the operation, maintenance, renewal and disposition of assets		P1.1	P1	
4	Activity	Process	Streamlining Asset Management		P1.2	P1	
5	Activity	Process	Business process improvement	measuring efficiency, improve efficiency	P2		
6	Activity	Process	Measuring Efficiency		P2.1	P2	
7	Activity	Process	Improving Efficiency		P2.2	P2	
8	Activity	Process	Customer service	onboarding new customers, service existing custo	P3		
9	Activity	Process	Onboarding new customers		P3.1	P3	
10	Activity	Process	Service existing customers		P3.2	P3	
11	Activity	Process	Customer feedback and complaints management		P3.3	P3	
12	Activity	Process	Delivery management process	automatic dispatch, vehicle tracking, delivery plann	P4		
13	Activity	Process	Automatic Dispatch		P4.1	P4	
14	Activity	Process	Vehicle Tracking		P4.2	P4	
15	Activity	Process	Delivery Planning		P4.3	P4	
16	Activity	Process	Finance process	budgeting, financial strategy, financial operations, f	P5		
17	Activity	Process	Budgeting		P5.1	P5	
18	Activity	Process	Financial Strategy		P5.2	P5	
19	Activity	Process	Financial Operations		P5.3	P5	
20	Activity	Process	Facilities Strategy		P5.4	P5	
21	Activity	Process	Facilities Operations		P5.5	P5	
22	Activity	Process	Financial Auditing		P5.6	P5	
23	Activity	Process	Human resource process	hiring employees, talent management, benefits man	P6		
24	Activity	Process	Hiring Employees		P6.1	P6	
25	Activity	Process	Talent Management		P6.2	P6	
26	Activity	Process	Benefits Management		P6.3	P6	
27	Activity	Process	Time and Attendance		P6.4	P6	
28	Activity	Process	Payroll		P6.5	P6	
29	Activity	Process	Marketing process	upstream marketing, downstream marketing, portfo	P7		
30	Activity	Process	Upstream Marketing		P7.1	P7	
31	Activity	Process	Downstream Marketing		P7.2	P7	

Figure 3-15. *Process list restructured*

We then go to Enterprise Architect where we do the following:

1. Change the import specification by checking "Preserve hierarchy."

2. Create a new folder "Process list restructured."

3. Reimport the restructured process list.

Nice! The import goes well, and the Project Browser shows the improved process list (Figure 3-16).

```
▲ ▣ₐ Model
  ▲ ▣ Function
    ▷ ▢ Process list
    ▲ ▢ Process list restructured
        ▤ Process list restructured
    ▲ ○ «process» Asset management
        ○ «process» Controlling and planning the operation, maintenance, renewal and disposition of assets
        ○ «process» Streamlining Asset Management
    ▲ ○ «process» Business process improvement
        ○ «process» Improving Efficiency
        ○ «process» Measuring Efficiency
    ▲ ○ «process» Customer service
        ○ «process» Customer feedback and complaints management
        ○ «process» Onboarding new customers
        ○ «process» Service existing customers
    ▲ ○ «process» Delivery management process
        ○ «process» Automatic Dispatch
        ○ «process» Delivery Planning
        ○ «process» Vehicle Tracking
    ▲ ○ «process» Finance process
        ○ «process» Budgeting
        ○ «process» Facilities Operations
        ○ «process» Facilities Strategy
        ○ «process» Financial Auditing
```

Figure 3-16. *Process list restructured in Project Browser*

In Chapter 5, we will discuss some techniques to reflect this structure in a diagram.

Updating Instead of Importing

We now have an improved model. The only thing lacking: descriptions for the new business processes. Also, it is better to replace the "descriptions" for the umbrella processes because the information is now twice in the model.

Suppose we need someone from Systemplar to fill in this list for us, and that person does not have access to Enterprise Architect. We can then give that person an export in spreadsheet format, asking for an update and then reimporting this information in Enterprise Architect.

During the time this person updates and adds information, we want to be able to work with the processes in Enterprise Architect.

This is where Enterprise Architect's round-tripping feature comes in handy. It works as follows:

1. Export the list of business processes with the key and the parent key provided by Enterprise Architect. This is a computer-produced string of letters and numbers, such that each element has a unique key. This export ID is unique for that export and different from the internal key Enterprise Architect creates for every element. It looks like this: CSV59260A5A. You include the key by checking "preserve hierarchy" in the export specification.

2. Update the export and import specifications to include the GUID, the Enterprise Architect internal ID. This is also a string of letters and numbers, this time with curly brackets around them.

3. Use spreadsheet software to update the descriptions and possibly the names of the processes, without changing the keys and the GUID.

4. Reimport the spreadsheet. In this step, Enterprise Architect will tell you it has "updated" elements that were already present, instead of "adding" them.

The round-trip export file looks like Figure 3-17 in a spreadsheet.

	A	B	C	D	E	F	G
1	Type	Stereotype	Name	Notes	GUID	CSV_KEY	CSV_PARENT_KEY
2	Activity	process	Finance process	budgeting, financial strategy, financial	{497B8A05-6EDA-4289-A22B-9B18BC1EA0A7}	CSV55631DDF	
3	Activity	process	Human resource process	hiring employees, talent management,	{FE144FFC-C3B3-491c-AEDB-F0B756A4BC85}	CSVBEA338B1	
4	Activity	process	Marketing process	upstream marketing, downstream mark	{734DD925-BF5E-4151-B84A-2F94D1732DC7}	CSV0D95E854	
5	Activity	process	Project management	starting and executing projects, organi	{23837FF0-5066-4f89-BA4E-95FC6CA99AE9}	CSVAA788926	
6	Activity	process	Product development	idea generation, concept developmen	{0C9A4CB8-7565-4278-A5FB-BDDFBD52A2CE}	CSVA9D6A30D	
7	Activity	process	Sales process	cold sales, upselling, sales automation	{FF97D7C1-907B-4717-B560-BF8737780040}	CSVB889C483	
8	Activity	process	Customer service	onboarding new customers, service ex	{CDAEFD1B-43D0-4f8f-B28E-CAA73B16EA93}	CSV4ADEDBC9	
9	Activity	process	Asset management	controlling and planning the operation,	{E0B85403-01EC-4e0b-8840-969804E1F5FD}	CSV8373F83A	
10	Activity	process	Procurement process	selecting vendors, establish payment	{6DA9F025-233B-48f1-9A6F-117378B1CB42}	CSVFF6F4B76	
11	Activity	process	Delivery management process	automatic dispatch, vehicle tracking, d	{08CC8BA4-53D7-4f97-B7FD-881C353E9A95}	CSV8EBC0386	
12	Activity	process	Business process improvemen	measuring efficiency, improve efficienc	{BF05CAE9-7453-47c2-8689-C2401BBCFB68}	CSV0EC471FF	
13	Activity	process	Portfolio Management	Keeping a list of products and services	{BADCC049-1980-42d4-97E0-EABB9C329E3F}	CSVFF976CBF	CSV0D95E854
14	Activity	process	Upstream Marketing		{83F3F705-40AC-4007-B244-119BC0DFA39B}	CSV68D06669	CSV0D95E854
15	Activity	process	Measuring Efficiency		{97F9D9CB-699B-4964-9A7B-8586E8720C2C}	CSV64CF6D1D	CSV0EC471FF
16	Activity	process	Vehicle Tracking		{87197742-5A28-4c10-A047-5634C9153F40}	CSV1EB9C9F8	CSV8EBC0386
17	Activity	process	Downstream Marketing		{9AFC8213-4256-474b-B17A-C5ADDA2E476E}	CSV156B6876	CSV0D95E854
18	Activity	process	Automatic Dispatch		{C643642D-F9B9-4f68-8686-7F4F6832B675}	CSV873AA568	CSV8EBC0386
19	Activity	process	Customer feedback and complaints management		{A03B6E84-BE9F-457f-96DB-D3F2A97B440C}	CSVFEAD0165	CSV4ADEDBC9
20	Activity	process	Benefits Management		{D6C433C4-F1B8-46d0-9BFD-BF7853FE3479}	CSVF704C1C8	CSVBEA338B1
21	Activity	process	Controlling and planning the operation, maintenance, renewal and disp	{80BFD4C8-693F-4445-BF08-6DEB9AE8C28C}	CSVAFB33A0F	CSV8373F83A
22	Activity	process	Delivery Planning		{991239B5-FF1E-4ee3-9773-D82510429DB1}	CSV23288A3B	CSV8EBC0386
23	Activity	process	Financial Operations		{3B51AF6B-B813-4ec8-8D28-0874687BC9BC}	CSV6F5146BD	CSV55631DDF
24	Activity	process	Financial Strategy		{DFCD3149-6A55-40e6-B3A2-C6B265A6C34F}	CSV20B9D4B2	CSV55631DDF
25	Activity	process	Streamlining Asset Management		{C918CBDB-3DB3-412b-AE73-BD324F6B6F66}	CSVB1C6C402	CSV8373F83A
26	Activity	process	Customer Relationships Management		{241E2E0E-EDB1-4980-A5C5-FB0967242C59}	CSV2E1E4DB8	CSV0D95E854
27	Activity	process	Facilities Operations		{CEB026AA-49FA-4c50-88D7-976DF2991C1B}	CSV536DFB68	CSV55631DDF
28	Activity	process	Onboarding new customers		{E2159909-150A-4256-B909-EF572FF79DC8}	CSVA87CEC59	CSV4ADEDBC9
29	Activity	process	Facilities Strategy		{64EFB53F-CA86-416a-B05A-B3CF11513930}	CSV3AE3106D	CSV55631DDF
30	Activity	process	Improving Efficiency		{70C4CD39-AB16-4c6a-BE85-D8A3E94F784B}	CSV8A3ECAE7	CSV0EC471FF
31	Activity	process	Service existing customers		{847074C3-4DEC-4cb0-9D7E-BDD34121C9E2}	CSV26735BC8	CSV4ADEDBC9
32	Activity	process	Financial Auditing		{DB1AB0A2-3E37-4da1-9894-916EF4E712B6}	CSVD726B1BD	CSV55631DDF
33	Activity	process	Hiring Employees		{772B2CFE-AE79-4f42-AFB1-7BB96BD7864B}	CSVF097AFE0	CSVBEA338B1
34	Activity	process	Budgeting	Yearly process starting in October and	{6A466493-4CAB-485d-89B9-7C90B48FAE52}	CSV02C2749E	CSV55631DDF

Figure 3-17. *Round-trip export*

Finding Elements

Now that our model has grown in size, we can no longer find elements just by scrolling through the Project Browser. Luckily, Enterprise Architect allows us to find elements with shortcuts. It pays to know these keyboard shortcuts: it will save you time and frustration.

Finding an Element from a Diagram in the Project Browser

Click the element and press Alt+G. The focus shifts to the Project Browser, and the corresponding element is selected (Figure 3-18).

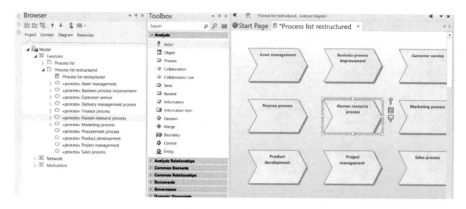

Figure 3-18. *Find an element from a diagram*

Alternatively, you can right-click the item and choose "Find" ➤ "In Project Browser."

Finding on Which Diagrams an Element Is Used

Click any element on a diagram to select it, then press Ctrl+U. Depending on where the element is used, this will happen:

- If the element is only present on the current diagram, nothing happens: the element stays selected.

- If the element is present in more than one diagram, a list of diagrams opens. You can then select a diagram and click "Open." The diagram opens and the corresponding element is selected.

Alternatively, you can right-click the element and choose "Find" ➤ "Find in all diagrams."

The same applies for the Project Browser. Click any element in the Project Browser and press Ctrl+U. If the element is an orphan (see the next section), an empty list appears. If the element appears on one diagram only, that diagram opens and the corresponding element is selected. If it appears on multiple diagrams, the list of diagrams is shown.

Alternatively, you can right-click the element and choose "Find in all diagrams" or "Locate in current diagram."

Finding Orphans

An orphan is an element that only sits in the Project Browser and that appears in no diagrams. There could be a reason to keep an orphan in the model, but usually orphans are the result of intense modeling sessions where there is no time to clean up the model.

The shortcut to open the model search window is easy to memorize: press Ctrl+F. To find orphaned elements, choose "Diagram Searches," then "Find Orphans" (Figure 3-19). Click the icon with the blue triangle.

	Object	Type	Stereotype	Scope	Status	Phase	Created	Modified
		Note		Public	Proposed	1.0	24/07/2022	24/07/2022
○	Asset manag...	Activity	process	Public	Proposed	1.0	24/09/2022	24/09/2022
○	Portfolio Man...	Activity	process	Public	Proposed	1.0	25/09/2022	25/09/2022
○	Upstream Ma...	Activity	process	Public	Proposed	1.0	25/09/2022	25/09/2022
○	Measuring Eff...	Activity	process	Public	Proposed	1.0	25/09/2022	25/09/2022
○	Vehicle Tracki...	Activity	process	Public	Proposed	1.0	25/09/2022	25/09/2022
○	Downstream ...	Activity	process	Public	Proposed	1.0	25/09/2022	25/09/2022
○	Automatic Di...	Activity	process	Public	Proposed	1.0	25/09/2022	25/09/2022
○	Customer fee...	Activity	process	Public	Proposed	1.0	25/09/2022	25/09/2022
○	Controlling a...	Activity	process	Public	Proposed	1.0	25/09/2022	25/09/2022
○	Delivery Plan...	Activity	process	Public	Proposed	1.0	25/09/2022	25/09/2022
○	Financial Ope...	Activity	process	Public	Proposed	1.0	25/09/2022	25/09/2022
○	Financial Stra...	Activity	process	Public	Proposed	1.0	25/09/2022	25/09/2022
○	Streamlining ...	Activity	process	Public	Proposed	1.0	25/09/2022	25/09/2022
○	Customer Rel...	Activity	process	Public	Proposed	1.0	25/09/2022	25/09/2022

Figure 3-19. *Finding orphans*

Deleting Elements

Deleting elements from a diagram is easy:

1. Select the element and press the "delete" key on the keyboard.

2. Or you can right-click the element and choose "Delete +<element_name>."

As we already discussed, this does not remove the element from the model. If you want to really delete an element from the model, you have to delete it in the Project Browser:

1. Right-click the element and choose "Delete + <element_name>."

2. If you want to delete multiple items at once, you have to select them all, then choose "Delete selected items" and confirm with "Yes to All" (Figure 3-20).

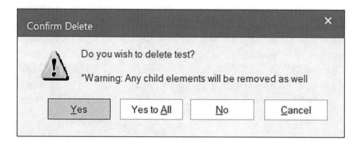

Figure 3-20. *Confirm delete*

Deleting elements will delete any child elements and diagrams and relationships with other elements as well.

Bookmarking Elements

During intensive modeling sessions, it is useful to keep track of to do's. Enterprise Architect has a nice feature that you can use for that: bookmarking elements.

Select any element and press Shift+Spacebar. A red triangle shows up on top of the element (Figure 3-21).

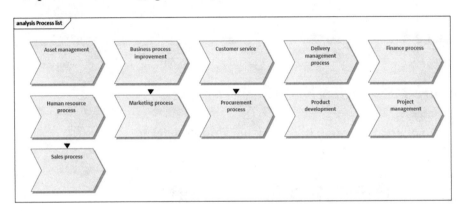

Figure 3-21. *Bookmarked elements*

This also works with multiselect: select more than one item by

1. Clicking them separately while holding the Ctrl or the Shift key pressed.

2. Dragging a "frame" around the elements to be selected.

3. Activating the diagram and pressing Ctrl+A if you want to select them all. Afterward, you can deselect individual elements with Ctrl+click.

Not only is this a nice visual way to keep track of work to do, but you can also search for bookmarked elements: press Ctrl+F to activate the search window, choose "Diagram Searches" and "Bookmarked Elements," and click the search icon (Figure 3-22).

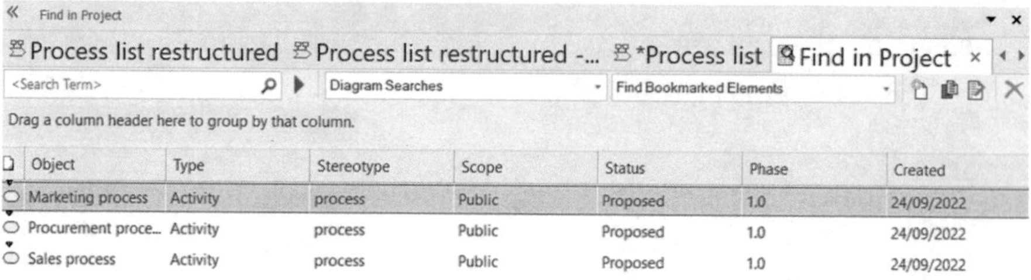

Figure 3-22. *Finding bookmarked elements*

To open an element in the list, just double-click it.

Element-Related Preferences

Enterprise Architect has multiple places where you can steer its behavior. One of these is the "Preferences" window. In the Ribbon, choose "Start" ➤ "Preferences" ➤ "Preferences...." A dialog window shows up (Figure 3-23). Choose "Objects" in the menu to the left.

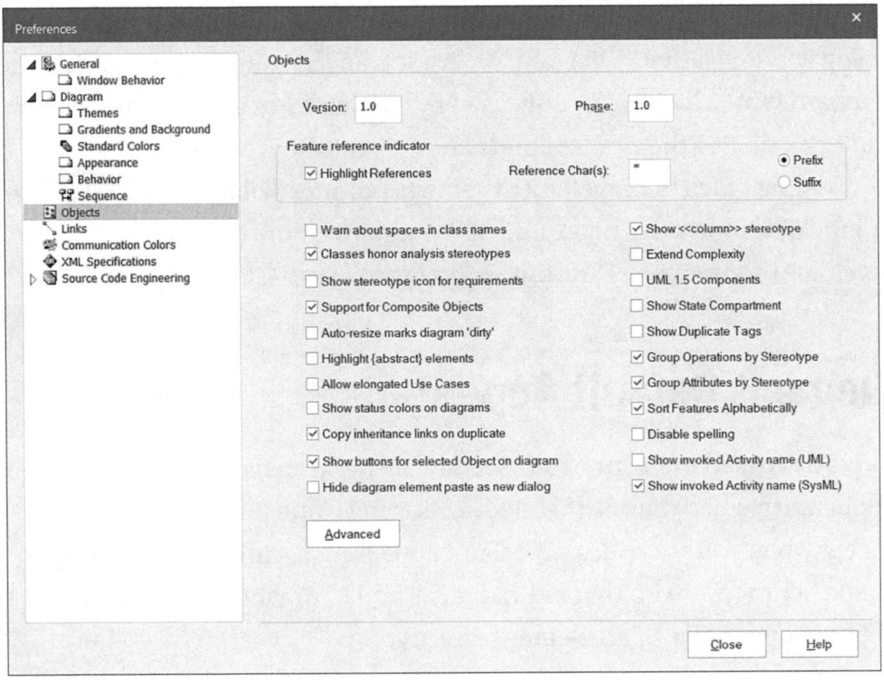

Figure 3-23. *Element-related preferences*

Only a handful of these settings are useful for our purposes:

- Version and phase: These are the default settings when an object is created.

- Support for composite objects: Should be "on" (the default setting). We will learn more about composing objects in Chapter 4.

- Show status colors on diagrams: Some elements, like requirements, can change color depending on their status (Proposed, Validated, Approved). This enhances the visual capabilities of diagrams. I suggest you turn this "on" (not the default setting).

Another place where element-related settings are stored is in the same dialog window under "Diagram" ➤ "Appearance." Here, you can define the standard font, which is not only used by elements but also on connectors and in notes. See the next chapters about connectors and notes.

The last place to find element settings is under "Diagram" ➤ "Standard Colors." These settings determine the standard colors for new elements, notes, and connectors. How this works speaks for itself.

Element Default Appearance

As we discussed in the previous section, elements have a default appearance when they are created. This is the same for all elements, except when you override this default appearance with a stereotype or a Shape Script (more on that in Chapters 8 and 9) or when you change the default appearance of an element directly.

Suppose, for example, that you want to give the location of Systemplars headquarters (Reims) a special look by coloring it yellow instead of the default beige. Each time Reims is added to a diagram, it will appear yellow instead of beige.

Open a diagram that shows the element, select it and press F4 or right-click and choose "Appearance" ➤ "Default Appearance..." (Figure 3-24).

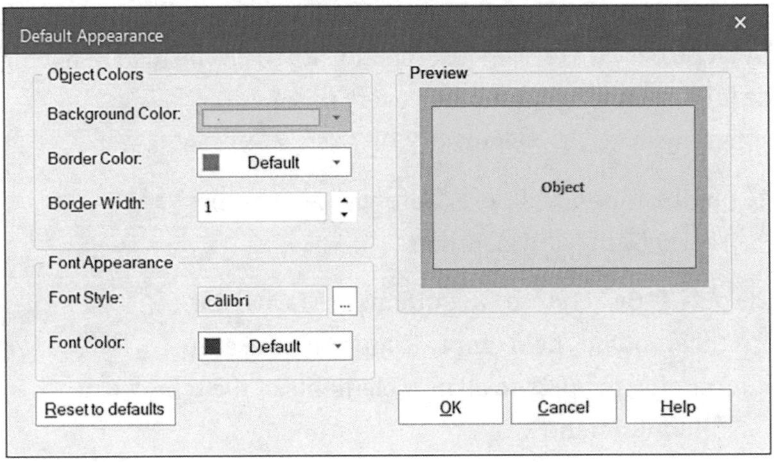

Figure 3-24. *Default appearance*

Notes

- If you want to change the appearance of an element on just one diagram, don't change the default appearance. Just change the color via the Design panel in the Ribbon.

- It is possible to change the default appearance of multiple elements at once. Select them on a diagram, right-click one of them, and choose "Appearance" ➤ "Default Appearance...."

Auto Names and Counters

A last useful feature of Enterprise Architect concerning elements is "auto names and counters." This allows you to apply a template to the names of a newly created element of a certain type and stereotype.

Suppose we gather requirements for the Enterprise Architecture "To Be" for Systemplar. Probably this list of requirements will be exported to a spreadsheet so that non-EA users can discuss these requirements. Wouldn't it be easy if they can just refer to "REQ123" instead of having to read the full text of the requirement every time?

Here's how to do this (Figure 3-25):

1. In the Ribbon, choose "Settings" ➤ "Settings" ➤ "Auto Name and Counters...."

2. As "Type," choose "Requirement." Leave the "Stereotype" field empty if you want the auto naming to apply to all new elements of the type "Requirement."

3. Type "REQ" in the "Prefix" field.

4. Type "00001" in the "Counter" field. This will start the counting at one and pad the number with zeroes to have a number that is at least five characters long.

5. Leave the "Suffix" empty.

6. Check "Apply on creation."

From now on, if you create an element of the type "Requirement," the name will automatically be filled in. You can, however, simply change this name by typing in some other text.

Note that you can have different auto names for a base class (a type like Requirement) and a base class with a specific stereotype (e.g., type="Requirement" and stereotype="Nonfunctional"). We will talk more about stereotypes in Chapter 8.

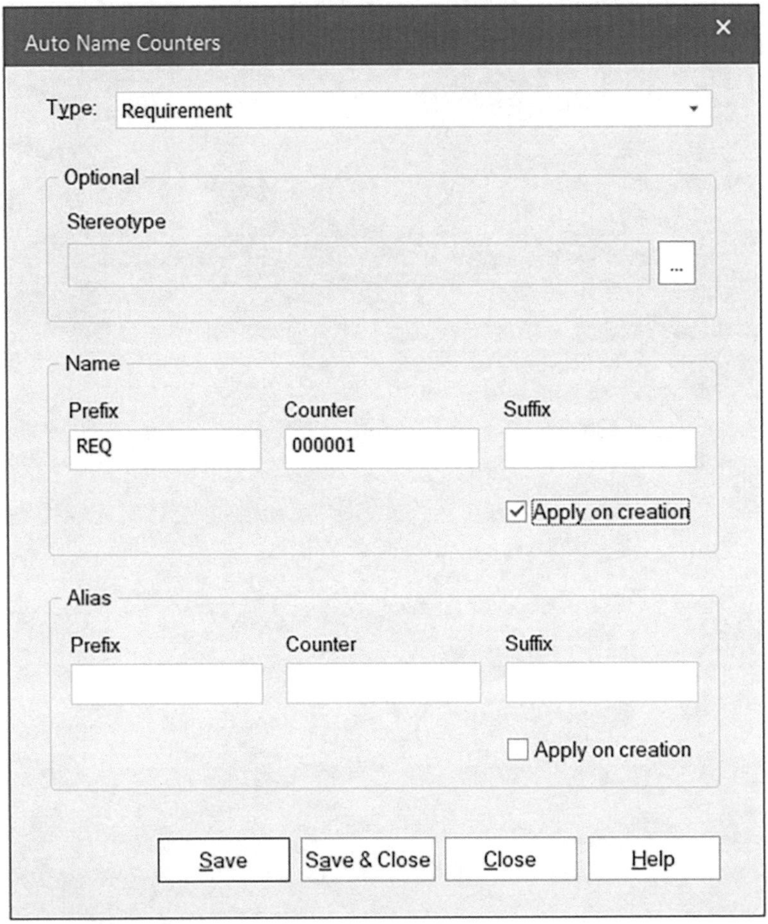

Figure 3-25. *Auto name and counters*

Summary

Elements are the "flesh" of any Enterprise Architect model: they contain
the actual information about the domain modeled. In this chapter, we
have seen various ways to add elements to the model, even from external
sources. We have also encountered the different properties of elements
and ways to change the default behavior of elements. The next chapter will
build on elements, since we are going to tie them together.

CHAPTER 4

Connecting Elements with Connectors

In this chapter, we learn that not all business processes take place at all Systemplar locations. Basically, the internal processes are centralized at the Systemplars headquarters in Reims, and the customer-facing processes take place in all offices. There are only a few exceptions, notably in Tunis, a recently acquired company that still runs some internal processes such as HR and asset management. We are now ready to start connecting the dots...

Case 4-1: Relating Business Processes to Locations

We put this information into SEAM, the Systemplar Enterprise Architecture Model. The diagram (Figure 4-1) is ugly, but we don't care: what's important is the model, and we will find a better way to represent this information later.

© Peter Doomen 2023
P. Doomen, *Introduction to SparxSystems Enterprise Architect*,
https://doi.org/10.1007/978-1-4842-9312-6_4

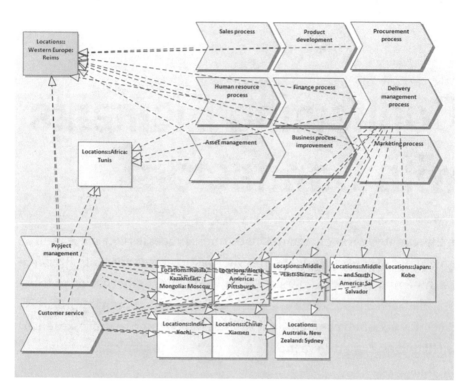

Figure 4-1. *Processes by locations*

Quickly Adding Links with the Quicklinker and Repeat Connector

What we did in five minutes would cost less experienced Enterprise Architect users at least half an hour. We will later reveal the fastest way to create lots of connectors: for now, we will discuss slower ways to connect elements.

We already mentioned the Quicklinker briefly in Chapter 2. Just to recapitulate, the Quicklinker shows up as an arrow at the top right of an element that is selected on a diagram. You then drag it either to another element on that diagram or to an empty space, in which case you get a dialog that allows you to create a new element.

Suppose we learn that some offices have subbranches, for example, in Reims where there is another office in the South of France near Marseille (Figure 4-2).

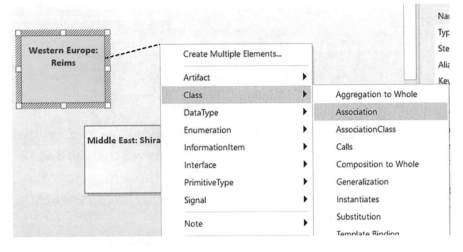

Figure 4-2. *The Quicklinker in action*

Simply drag the Quicklinker to an empty space on the diagram, release the mouse button, and choose "Class" ➤ "Association." A class will be created, and it will be connected to the Reims class with an association link. You only have to type in its name "Marseille."

If you have more than one new item to create and connect, you can choose "Create Multiple Elements…" in the context menu of the Quicklinker (Figure 4-3).

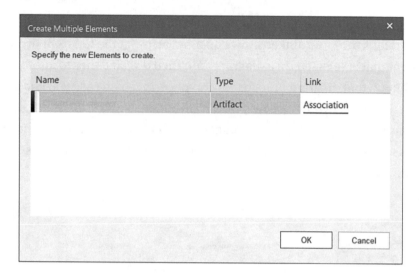

Figure 4-3. *Create multiple elements*

Just set the type field to "Class" and the link field to "Association." Then start typing the names, confirm with "OK," and they will be created and linked to the source element.

Neat! But what if you have multiple existing elements that you want to connect with each other?

Let's, for example, create "Associate" relations between all offices and headquarters. Use the Quicklinker to create one relationship (Figure 4-4).

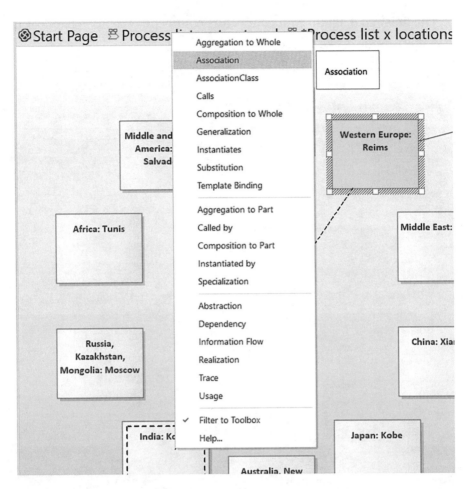

Figure 4-4. *Linking existing elements*

Here, we used the Quicklinker to link Reims and India:Kochi with an association relation. Now just press F3 (Repeat Connector) and drag from the middle of the Reims class to another class. No more pop-ups and no need to use the Quicklinker. That is fast! But can we go even faster? Sure. But let's save the best part for last. First, we will discuss other ways to link elements, relationship properties, and some other handy tools that come with Enterprise Architect.

The finished diagram with connectors connecting the branch offices to headquarters looks like Figure 4-5.

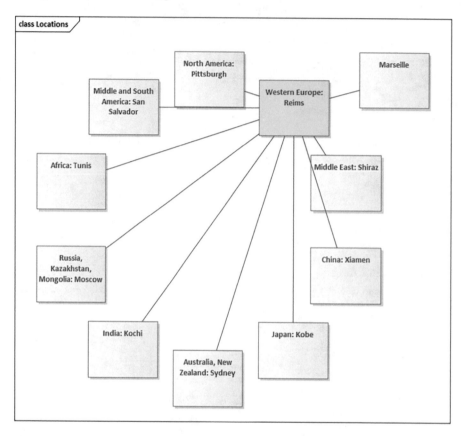

Figure 4-5. *Location diagram with connectors*

Creating Links from the Project Browser

Another way to add a link from one element to another is by using the context menu in the Project Browser. Click "Add" ➤ "Create Link" and select the right target type in the dialog box, then choose the element(s) and confirm with "OK" (Figure 4-6). Although selecting the target type is a bit clumsy, this is actually a very fast way to add multiple relationships to an element, provided these elements are of the same type. Just use Ctrl or Shift while clicking and you can create hundreds of links in a matter of seconds.

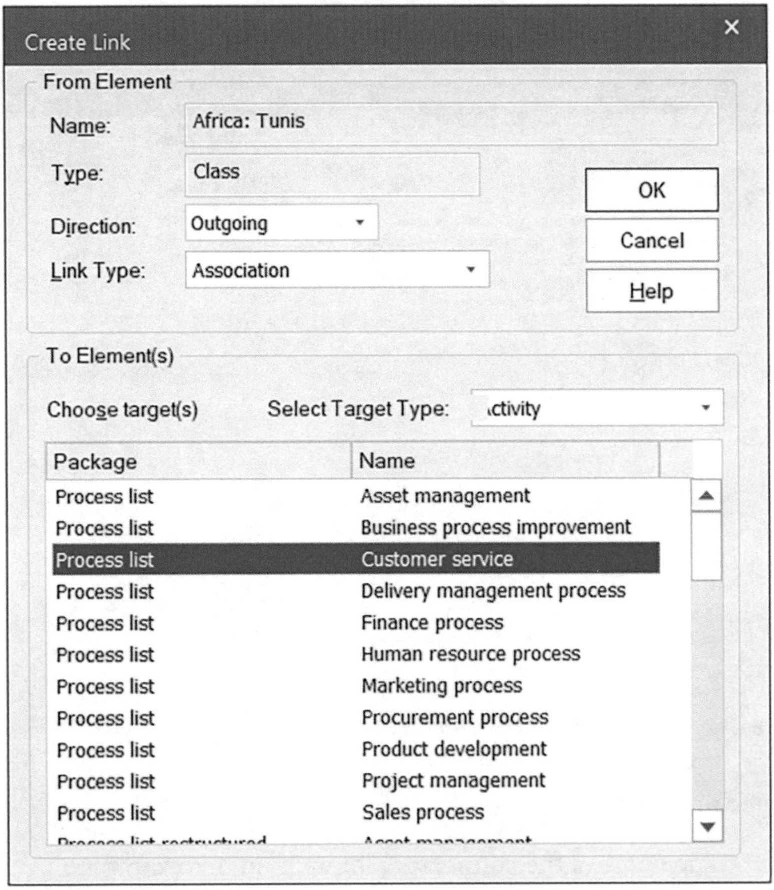

Figure 4-6. *Create link*

Relationship Properties

Like elements, relationships have properties where you can store information. The easiest way to open the properties window is by double-clicking the relation on a diagram (Figure 4-7).

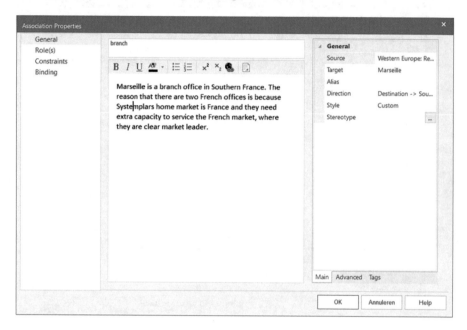

Figure 4-7. *Association properties*

Some important properties include

- The name of the connector ("branch" in this example): You can leave this blank if you don't want a text to appear on the link.

- A description: This can also be blank.

- Information about the source and the target, so you can quickly see which elements are connected by the relation.

- An alias: A secondary name.

- A direction: Unspecified, both directions, or from one element to the other. If you specify a direction, the link will show an arrow on the diagram.

- A style: This changes the way the connector appears on a diagram. See the next section.

- A stereotype: Similar to the element stereotypes, relation stereotypes can influence the behavior and appearance of the connector. We will deal with stereotypes in Chapter 8.

Connector Styles

On diagrams with lots of connectors, things can get cluttered. Therefore, you can choose how connectors should behave when they meet elements and other connectors.

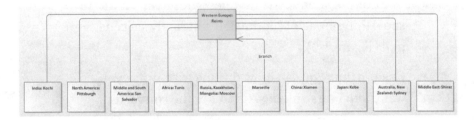

Figure 4-8. *Connector style rounded orthogonal*

You can set the connector style via the relationship properties or by right-clicking the connector on a diagram and then clicking "Line Style" + the preferred style (Figure 4-8).

If you want to apply this style to other connectors in the same diagram, just select the connector, right-click, and choose "Apply Line Style on Diagram" ➤ "Connectors of the Same Type."

How connectors look can have a big impact on the readability of a diagram. Here is the same diagram but with the connector styles set to "autorouting" (Figure 4-9). I agree that this Enterprise Architect feature needs rework.

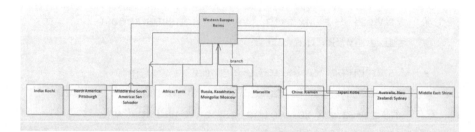

Figure 4-9. *Autorouting does not always give a visually appealing representation*

The major styles are as follows:

- Direct: A straight line from the source to the target element.

- Autorouting: Enterprise Architect tries to find a way to show the connector "optimally," but rarely succeeds in that (Figure 4-9).

- Custom line: You can draw the line exactly like you want with line segments. Ctrl+click the connector where you want a break to appear. Every break, represented by a small white square, can individually be positioned.

- Bezier: A curve that can be bent by dragging the inflection handle.

- Tree: Either horizontal or vertical, resembles an org chart.

- Lateral: Also horizontal or vertical, gives a tree-like view but with connectors that overlap. This can also significantly reduce clutter since there are less lines on the diagram.

- Orthogonal – square or rounded: Another tree-like style, but the option to round off the edges of the connectors often gives a smooth look.

After having changed the style of a connector, you might need to improve the layout by dragging the connector around or by dragging one of its endpoint handles.

Docking and Nesting Elements

By docking or nesting elements, you do not create a real relationship in the Enterprise Architect sense of the word. Yet docked or nested elements get "connected" somehow, albeit loosely.

We will talk about docked elements in the next chapter, since this is actually a diagramming technique that is useful for working with similar elements on diagrams and to make diagrams easier to read.

Nested elements we already encountered when we imported the processes in the previous chapter. The "parent-child" relationship shows in the browser, since the children are visually under their parent process.

Now it is time to improve on that. Instead of having the relationship between the parent process and its children implicit, we will explicitly model it by adding relationships from the child to its parent.

For reasons that will become clear in the next chapter, we will use a "composition" relation to indicate that the parent process is actually an umbrella. Here is how to do it:

1. Create a new diagram, and drag the first parent process on it. Also, drag its children on the diagram.

2. Open the "class" toolbox by clicking the icon with the three horizontal lines in the Toolbox window.

3. Click the "composition" relation in the toolbox, and drag from the first child to the parent on the diagram.

4. Press "F3" (Repeat Connector) and add the "composition" relationship for the other children.

5. Remove the elements from the diagram, and continue with the next processes.

After each step, the result looks like Figure 4-10.

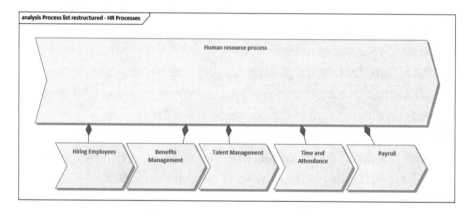

Figure 4-10. *Creating a hierarchy for the processes*

Relationship-Related Preferences

Like with elements, relationships have some preferences (Figure 4-11) that the user can set to make working with Enterprise Architect easier.

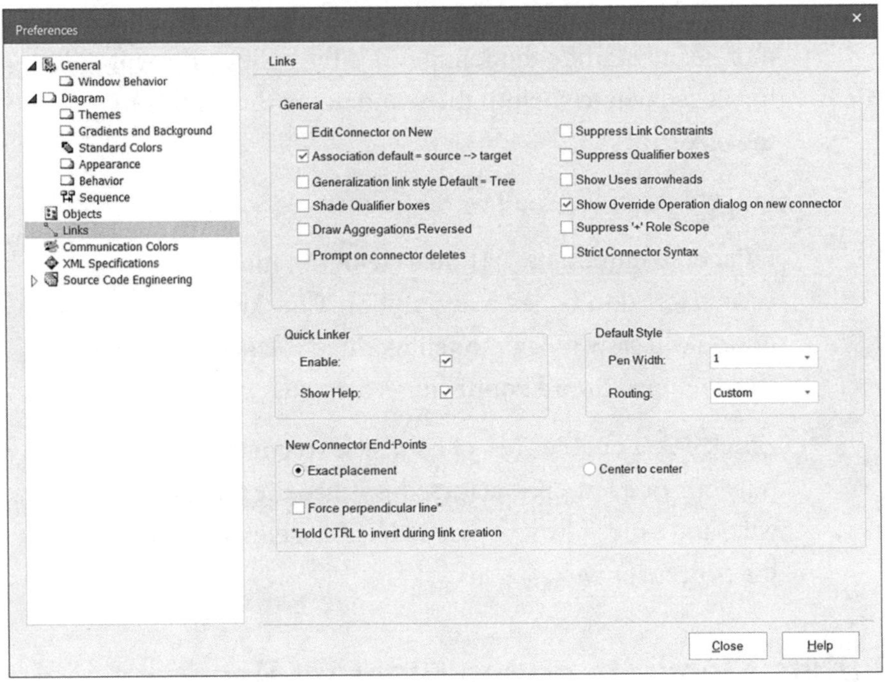

Figure 4-11. *Link preferences*

Some of the default settings may suit people who use Enterprise Architect for technical work, but are less suited for our purposes. I suggest you change these settings:

- Association default = source --> target

- Prompt on connector deletes: I create and delete connectors a lot, and I don't need Enterprise Architect showing me a warning each time I do that.

- Strict Connector Syntax: This might be useful if you use Enterprise Architect for simulations or code generations, but it makes less sense for our work.

- New Connector End-Points: Exact placement gives you more control while modeling, since the connectors will be placed where you put them and not in the middle of the element.

For some settings, the default works for me:

- Edit connector on new: Unlike elements, most connectors don't need a description. Checking this option will slow down modeling, since you get a dialog window each time a connector is created.

- Quick linker enable: Yes, of course! If you need to create only one or a few connectors, this is usually the fastest way, and especially if you need to create elements in the process as well.

Putting Elements on the Diagram Based on Links

A powerful feature of Enterprise Architect is the ability to create diagrams based on the multidimensional model structure. Say, for example, we want to create a diagram that shows all of the processes that run in the Tunis office (as you remember, the big exception to the Systemplar policy of having internal processes only in headquarters).

First, we drag the class "Africa: Tunis" to a new diagram. Then we right-click it and choose "Insert related elements...." A dialog window shows up (Figure 4-12).

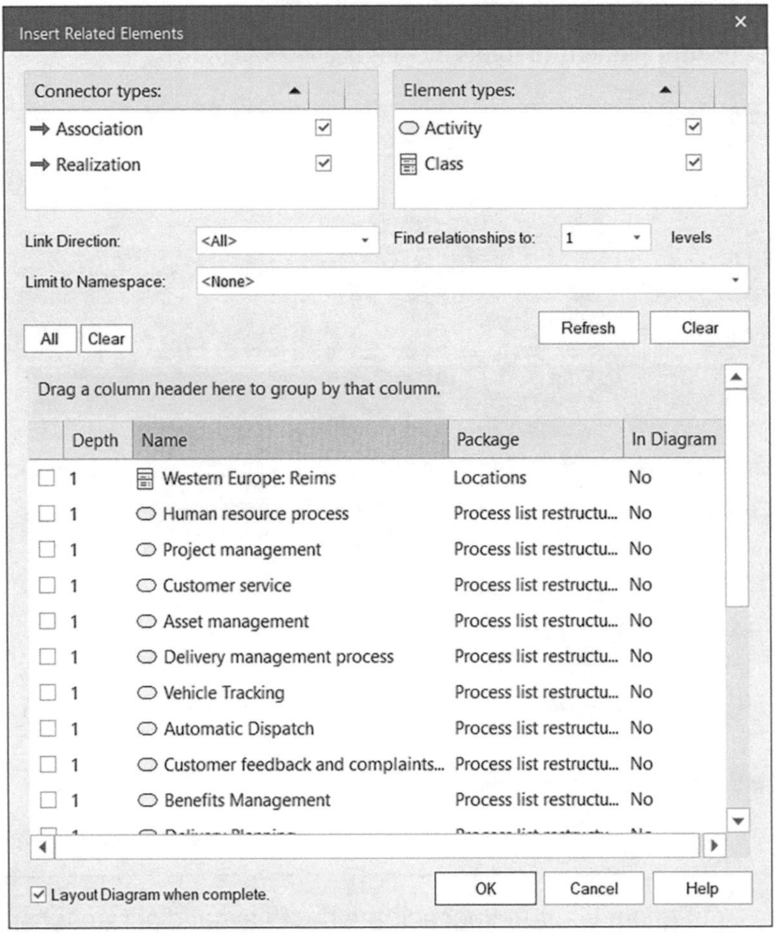

Figure 4-12. *Insert related elements*

Now you can simply select the items you want to appear on the diagram and close with "OK," but there are smarter ways of doing this.

Since we want all processes to appear, but not the headquarters element, you could limit the element type to "Activity" (since that is the base class we use for processes). Click "Refresh" when you have deselected "Class" at the top right. Click "All" on top of the element list, and confirm with "OK."

The same holds for limiting "Connectors" to a certain type. The resulting diagram looks like Figure 4-13.

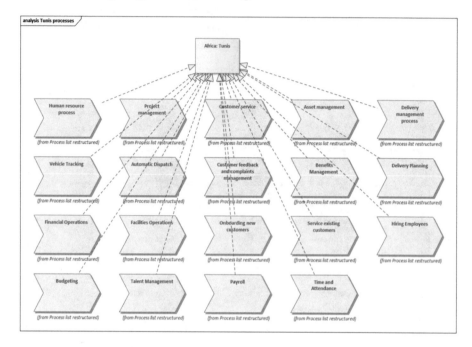

Figure 4-13. *Processes in Tunis*

Note   You might want to uncheck the box "Layout diagram when complete" in the "Insert Related Elements" dialog window and manually lay out the diagram. We will talk more about diagram layouts and removing clutter in the next chapter.

More Options

There are a few more options that you can use to quickly get the results that you want:

- Link direction: The default is "all," but you can choose to limit the element list to incoming or outgoing relationships.

- Find relationships to X levels: If you pick a number higher than one, the element list will grow, because it will also contain elements that are deeper in the relationship structure. If element A is connected to B and B to C, and you insert related elements up to two levels from A, C will be shown as well.

- Limit to namespace: You can define a part of the model as a namespace, then use this definition to limit the element list to elements that belong to this namespace. More on namespaces later.

- Drag a column header to group by that column: Quickly group elements by dragging the relevant column header to the top.

Namespaces

If the model is big and has heavily interconnected elements, you can work with namespaces to limit the number of elements that show up when adding related elements.

To set a namespace root, select the package you want to function as the namespace root, then click "Develop" ➤ "Options" in the Ribbon and choose "Set Package as Namespace Root" (Figure 4-14).

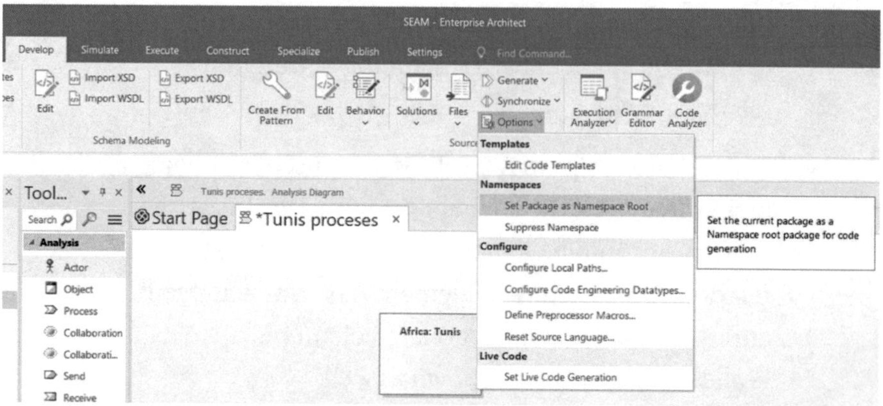

Figure 4-14. *Setting a namespace root*

"Suppress Namespace" removes this.

In our case, it makes sense to add each of the top-level packages as a namespace root.

To consult which namespaces exist in the model, go to "Settings" ➤ "Settings" in the Ribbon and choose "Namespace Roots" (Figure 4-15).

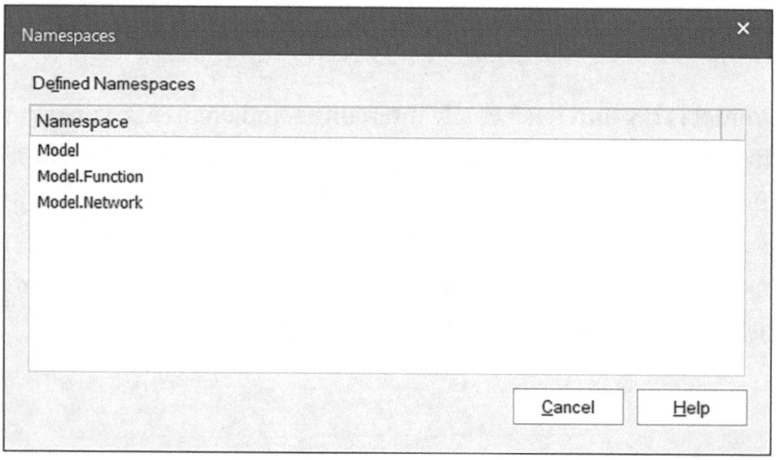

Figure 4-15. *Defined namespaces*

Also, the Project Browser reveals which packages are namespace roots: they get a little red corner icon at their bottom right.

The Traceability Window

Enterprise Architect has got another trick up its sleeve for adding related elements to a diagram: the Traceability window. Open it in the Ribbon by selecting "Design" ➤ "Trace." Anytime you select an element, in a diagram or in the Project Browser, its related elements are shown here. Browse through the list, and use the context menu to add a related element to the current diagram.

Figure 4-16 shows an example.

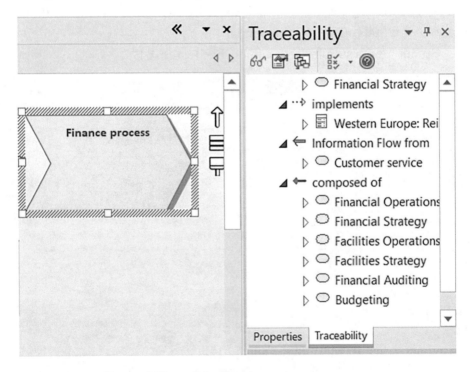

Figure 4-16. *Traceability of the finance process*

Adding Information to Connectors: Notes and Information Flows

Let's return to our Systemplar case to illustrate how one can add notes and information flows to connectors.

We learn that there are important business concepts used by Systemplar employees to describe their business, such as Customer, Product, and Service. It is easy to guess that things like "Invoice" and "Order" will play a role as well.

These concepts relate to the "Data" column of the Zachman Framework. At its highest level, it is just a list of things the business cares about. Deeper layers would add more structure to that, for example, to clarify the relation between orders, invoices, and customers or the different types of products offered by Systemplar.

But for now, a simple list would do, like Figure 4-17.

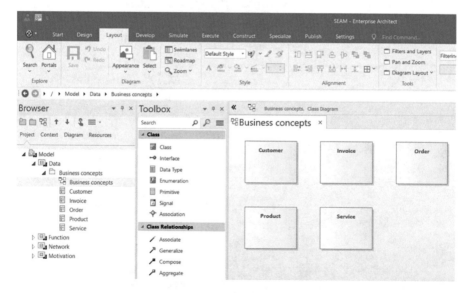

Figure 4-17. *Adding business concepts*

We can now return to the process list, where we can use the newly created business concepts to add a bit more structure to the processes.

We add three business processes to the diagram: the sales process, customer service, and the finance process. Then we add an information flow between the sales process and customer service (Figure 4-18).

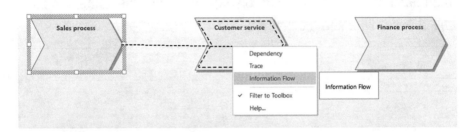

Figure 4-18. *Adding an information flow*

A dialog "Information Items Conveyed" pops up (Figure 4-19). Via the "Add" button, we add "Order" from the business concepts to the information flow. We do the same with "invoice" between the customer service process and the finance process.

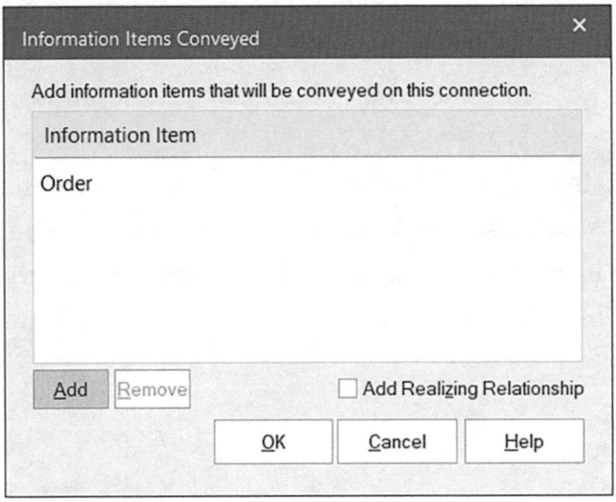

Figure 4-19. *Information items conveyed*

The result is a simple, but already insightful, diagram (Figure 4-20) that we can use to understand how the different processes work together at Systemplar.

Note   If you want to know the location in the Project Browser of an information item on a connector on a diagram, use the context menu and choose "Find items conveyed."

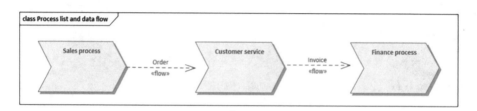

Figure 4-20. *Linking processes*

However, we still are not too sure about the last step. It depends on how Systemplar runs their business: Do they wait until the customer has been served before sending an invoice, or does the invoice get generated as soon as the order has been made?

Therefore, we add a note to the connector so that somebody could clarify this.

To achieve that, right-click the connector and choose "Attach note or constraint...." A dialog shows that lets you connect the note to multiple connectors, if needed. Confirm with OK, then double-click the empty note and type in some text. The resulting diagram is shown in Figure 4-21.

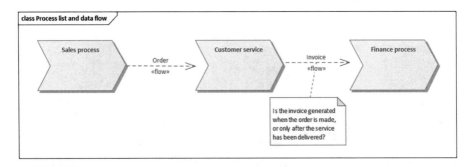

Figure 4-21. *Adding a note to an information flow*

The Relationship Matrix

We are ready for the final part of this chapter, where we will reveal how we spent just five minutes to connect the locations and the processes, instead of drawing all the connectors separately. We use the Relationship Matrix for that. But as we will see, there is a lot more power to this Relationship Matrix than just for mass creation of relationships.

The Relationship Matrix (Figure 4-22) is a matrix view on the model. It can show two packages, one on the vertical axis and one on the horizontal, with the cells indicating existing relationships. These packages can even be the same, in case there are relationships between elements in the same package.

To open the Relationship Matrix, click a package in the Project Browser (e.g., Process List) and go to the Ribbon: "Design" ➤ "Package" ➤ "Open as source." Then drag the target package ("Locations") from the Project Browser to the Target field in the Relationship Matrix, or use the three-dotted icon to select it with a dialog window.

Select as type "all" for both the source and the target. As a link type, choose "Realization." Now Ctrl+click or Shift+click cells where you want to create a connector, right-click, and choose "Create new relationship" ➤ "UML:Realization." In the screenshot, you see both the action and the result: the green cells with blue arrows indicate existing relationships; the blue cells will get a new relationship after confirmation.

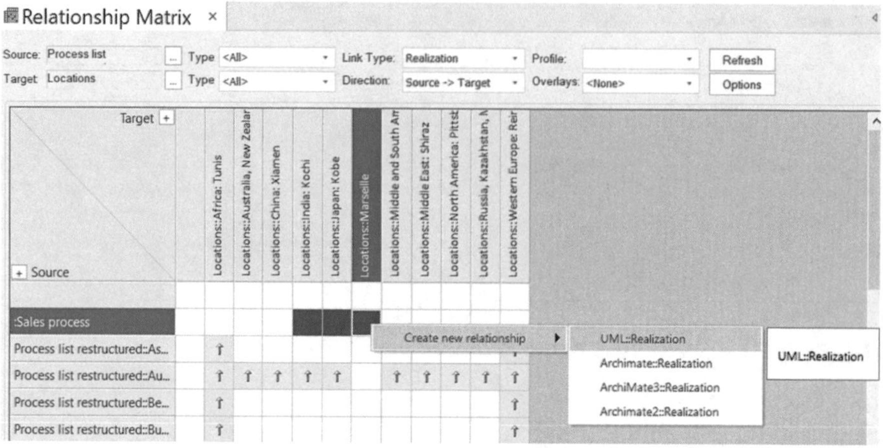

Figure 4-22. *Creating relationships with the Relationship Matrix*

Saving Settings

Quite possibly, you will need the same configuration of source and target package and types again, so it is a good idea to save these settings. Click "Options" ➤ "Profiles" ➤ "Save as new profile." Give the profile a name such as "Process x Location" so that you know what it stands for. The profile will be added to the Profiles list box on top of the Relationship Matrix.

Matrix Options

When you click "Options" ➤ "Options," the Matrix Options dialog appears. You can set these options:

- Include source/target children: Our process list has umbrella processes and children of these. By unchecking this option, you can hide the children.

- Sort Axes: Sort both axes alphabetically or leave them in the order they appear in the Project Browser.

- Show Package Names: Uncheck to increase the readability of the Relationship Matrix, since the package name is already indicated in the source and target field.

- Use Element Alias if available: Instead of using the element's regular name, use its alias.

- Show Level Numbering if available: Numbers the elements if this feature is turned on in the Project Browser. To activate this, click "Design" ➤ "Manage" in the Ribbon and choose "Level Numbering."

- Highlight source/target elements without relationships: Check this box to quickly see gaps, like locations where nothing happens.

Exporting the Matrix

Once the matrix is created, you can export it as a metafile or as a png (both graphical formats). The other option is export to csv (Figure 4-23), and that does exactly what the name says. Click "Options" ➤ "Matrix" to find the export options.

	A	B	C	D	E	F	G	H	I	J	K	L
1		Western Euro▸	Russia, Kaza▸	North Americ▸	Middle East: ▸	Middle and S▸	Marseille	Japan: Kobe	India: Kochi	China: Xiame▸	Australia, Ne▸	Africa: Tunis
2	Vehicle Tracking	X	X	X	X	X		X	X	X	X	X
3	Upstream Marketing	X										
4	Time and Attendance	X										X
5	Talent Management	X										X
6	Streamlining Asset Management	X										
7	Service existing customers	X	X	X	X	X		X	X	X	X	X
8	Sales process	X										
9	Project management	X	X	X	X	X		X	X	X	X	X
10	Product development	X										
11	Procurement process	X										
12	Portfolio Management	X										
13	Payroll	X										X
14	Onboarding new customers	X	X	X	X	X		X	X	X	X	X
15	Measuring Efficiency	X										
16	Marketing process	X										
17	Improving Efficiency	X										
18	Human resource process	X										X
19	Hiring Employees	X										X
20	Financial Strategy	X										
21	Financial Operations	X										X
22	Financial Auditing	X										
23	Finance process	X										
24	Facilities Strategy	X										
25	Facilities Operations	X										X
26	Downstream Marketing	X										
27	Delivery Planning	X	X	X	X	X		X	X	X	X	X
28	Delivery management process	X	X	X	X	X		X	X	X	X	X
29	Customer service	X	X	X	X	X		X	X	X	X	X
30	Customer Relationships Management	X										
31	Customer feedback and complaints mar▸	X	X	X	X	X		X	X	X	X	X
32	Controlling and planning the operation, r▸	X										
33	Business process improvement	X										
34	Budgeting	X										X
35	Benefits Management	X										X
36	Automatic Dispatch	X	X	X	X	X		X	X	X	X	X
37	Asset management	X										X

Figure 4-23. *Export to csv*

Working with Overlays

Exporting becomes even more functional if we use overlays. Suppose we want to convey information about how well a process is organized in each of the locations. We define an overlay "ProcessQuality." Select <New Overlay…> in the overlay field (Figure 4-24).

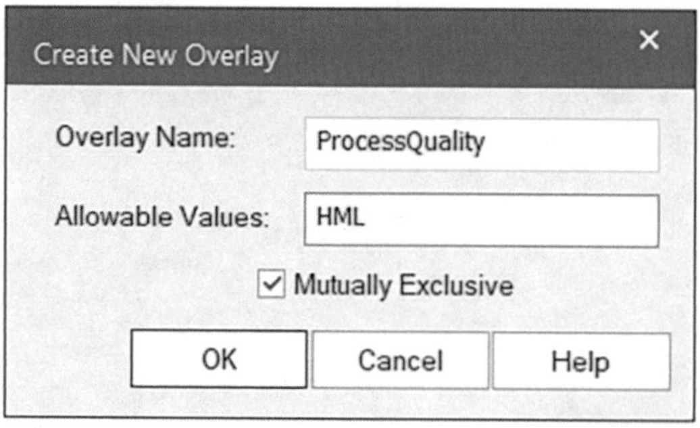

Figure 4-24. *Create new overlay*

Give it a name ("ProcessQuality") and allowable values HML for High, Medium, Low. These are mutually exclusive so we leave that box checked.

Confirm with "OK." We can now right-click a cell in the Relationship Matrix and choose "Apply Overlay." We then get a dialog window where we can indicate the process quality for this location.

Not only will the overlay value replace the arrow in the Relationship Matrix, but also the csv export will reflect the overlay value rather than the standard "X" (Figure 4-25).

	A	B	C	D	E	F	G	H	I	J	K	L
1		Western Eu	Russia, Ka	North Amer	Middle East	Middle and	Marseille	Japan: Kob	India: Kochi	China: Xian	Australia, N	Africa: Tunis
2	Vehicle Tracking	H	H	M	M	L		L	H	H	H	M
3	Upstream Marketing	H										
4	Time and Attendance	M										M
5	Talent Management	M										H
6	Streamlining Asset Management	M										

Figure 4-25. *Export with overlay*

This feature is used in other contexts as well. Two more examples:

- For IT systems, a CRUD matrix is a well-known tool. Here, the values are not mutually exclusive: it is perfectly possible and indeed quite common that an application that creates data also can read, update, and delete that same data.

- A RACI matrix is used in organizational design to indicate who is responsible or accountable, who gets informed, and who is consulted. Also here values are not mutually exclusive.

Once an overlay is created for a matrix, the context menu of "create relationship" is extended with "create relationship with overlay."

Notes on overlays

- It is possible to have more than one overlay on the same matrix.

- Overlays are stored as tagged values. We will work with tagged values in Chapter 8.

Summary

In this chapter, we created connectors between elements in several different ways. We also explored some options to use these connectors to show information. The next chapter will discuss the creation and layout of diagrams in more detail.

CHAPTER 5

Using Diagrams to Present Information

We from IT are used to work with composite models. Enterprise architecture models are simple.

—John Zachman

In this chapter, you'll see how to refine cluttered diagrams into something more elegant and fit for presentation – and much more about creating and layouting diagrams, including

- Manual and autolayout

- Copying diagrams

- Diagram types

- How to add colors and legends to diagrams and how to generate a heat map from that

- Using diagram filters to show or hide information

- Work with different views such as Gantt charts and specifications and other special diagrams

- Working with diagrams in an efficient way

© Peter Doomen 2023
P. Doomen, *Introduction to SparxSystems Enterprise Architect*,
https://doi.org/10.1007/978-1-4842-9312-6_5

Case 5-1: A Business Process Model

Remember the cluttered process diagram we created? Its content was good, but the presentation could be improved a lot (Figure 5-1). That is exactly what we are going to do.

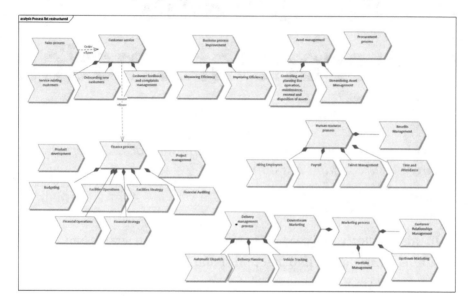

Figure 5-1. *A cluttered process diagram*

What a mess! The only advantage is that reviewers will understand it is still a "work in progress." Nevertheless, let's spend ten minutes restructuring the diagram. The result is shown in Figure 5-2.

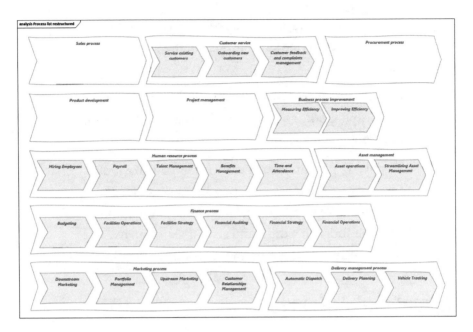

Figure 5-2. *Less cluttered process diagram*

Here is what to do:

- Resize the umbrella processes so they have the same height and can contain the underlying processes, which are also the same size. For one process, this meant we have to shorten its name: we move the long name to the description and change the name to "asset operations."

- Color these umbrella processes white, a color that is only valid for this diagram.

- Move the processes in the umbrella processes. As we saw in Chapter 4, the connectors automatically vanish.

- Hide the connectors between the processes of sales, finance, and service since this is not the focus of this diagram.

- Arrange the processes so they would fit on a page in landscape mode, and align the objects so their left and top would be the same.

- Finally, we give the diagram a whiteboard-like look – this conveys the message "work in progress, feedback welcome." We can copy the diagram to the clipboard with the shortcut Ctrl+B and send it via email to a bunch of Systemplar employees, asking for feedback.

Manual and Autolayout

Enterprise Architect has a feature that allows you to automatically lay out diagrams. This works for simple diagrams with not too many different elements and relationships.

To autolayout a diagram, go to the Ribbon and choose "Layout" ➤ "Diagram Layout." This is what happens to the business process "umbrella" model when you choose "Apply Default Layout" (Figure 5-3).

Figure 5-3. *Apply default layout*

This is not too bad: elements that have a relationship between each other are placed nearby, and overall the diagram looks good.

You can also try your luck and select the elements to undergo layouting, then click "Layout selected elements" in the context menu.

Other Diagram Layout Options

Other diagram options include box, circle, and ellipse, which do what you would expect: they arrange the elements in a rectangular, circular, or ellipsoid format. The first is ideal if you have a diagram without relationships (basically just a list of elements), the other ones when there are lots of connectors without a clear structure.

Still other options are

- Converge and diverge: Enterprise Architect pulls the elements closer to each other or the reverse.

- Autoroute: Enterprise Architect reroutes connectors so they don't overlap with elements.

- Spring: Enterprise Architect reorders elements so their connectors don't overlap.

- Fan relations: Enterprise Architect reorders the elements around the selected element such that its relations are organized around it.

As usual, you should try out these options for yourself to really understand what they do.

Layout Tools

If you want to have more control on the autolayout, you can open the Layout Tools window which will by default stick to the right side of the Enterprise Architect main window (Figure 5-4).

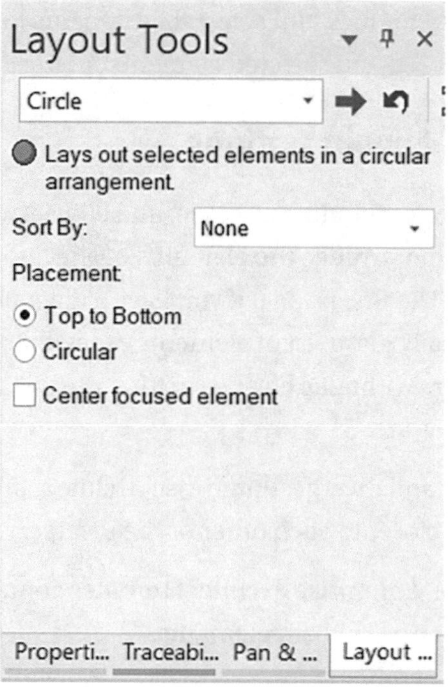

Figure 5-4. *Layout tools*

Depending on the layout type (box, circle, etc.), you get different layouting options. These are the most common ones:

- Sort by: For example, if you want to sort the items by their name, choose "Name (Ascending)."

- Center focused element (for circular or ellipsoid layouting): If there is one element that has many more relations than the others, put this one in the middle and it will greatly simplify your diagram.

- Automatically distribute/specify distribution: For rectangular layouts. Specify how many columns you want to use, or let Enterprise Architect decide on that.

Manual Layouting

For complicated diagrams with lots of relations, you can either start from an automatic layout and then improve it with manual layouting or start manually layouting right away.

Here are some useful hints and tools:

- Select multiple elements (by holding the Ctrl or Shift button while clicking them or by dragging over them) and right-click a correctly sized one. Then choose "Make same height and width."

- The same goes for aligning tops, bottoms, rights, lefts, or centers (Figure 5-5). Remember that the reference element is always the last one you selected. If needed, deselect and reselect the reference element. Instead of right-clicking an item, you can also use the buttons on the Ribbon ("Layout" ➤ "Alignment").

- To get the same space between each pair of neighboring elements, choose "Space evenly," then "across" (horizontal) or "down" (vertical).

- If items overlap, you might want to change their Z-order so that the smallest element is still visible. Select an element, right-click it, and choose "Z-order" and then the move you want it to make: "back" for one move to the bottom, "bottom" to make it the least visible element, and "front" and "top" to make it more visible. Also here you can use the buttons on the Ribbon.

- To hide a connector on a diagram, right-click it and choose "Visibility" ➤ "Hide Connector." To make a hidden connector visible again, select one of both elements and open its properties window. In the "Links" tab, right-click the link and choose "Show Relationship." Note that this is separate for each diagram. You can also hide the link from all other diagrams except this one by choosing "Visibility" ➤ "Hide Connector in Other Diagrams" from the context menu.

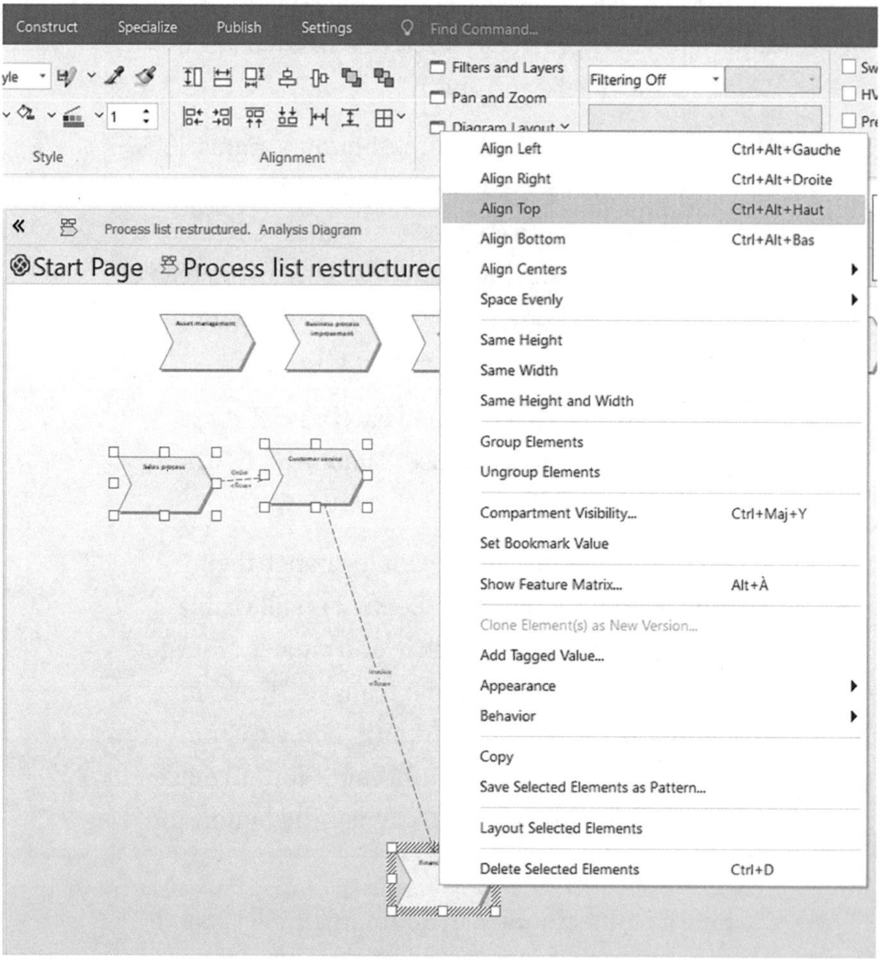

Figure 5-5. *Aligning the tops*

Copying Diagrams

Sometimes, it makes sense to copy an existing diagram, for example, when you want to show the same information presented slightly differently.

To copy a diagram, right-click it in the Project Browser and choose "Copy" ➤ "Copy Diagram." Right-click the package in the Package Browser where the copy should be added, and choose "Paste" ➤ "As new diagram."

A dialog pops up that wants you to choose the type of copy:

- Shallow: Only the diagram is copied. The elements are pasted as a link, so they don't get duplicated. This is probably what you want.

- Deep: All visual elements on the diagram get copied along with it. I can't think of more than two good use cases for this. One might be GUI design, where you want more than one version of the same interface design to be presented to a user.

- Smart: Identical to "Deep" but it copies every element that is "owned" by the diagram. Same remark: Hard to think of good use cases for this.

Diagram Types

Every diagram has a "type": the one that you choose when you create it. Depending on the diagram type, a toolbox is activated when you open it, containing the tools you most probably need when working on that diagram.

This toolbox consists of typical elements (such as class, data type, interface, etc., for a class diagram) and also a set of typical connectors (like associate, generalize, and compose for class diagrams). What if you made a mistake when creating the diagram? Can you still change its type?

Sure!

Just go to the Ribbon and select "Design" ➤ "Diagram" ➤ "Options" ➤ "Change Type..." and choose the appropriate diagram type in the dialog that appears (Figure 5-6).

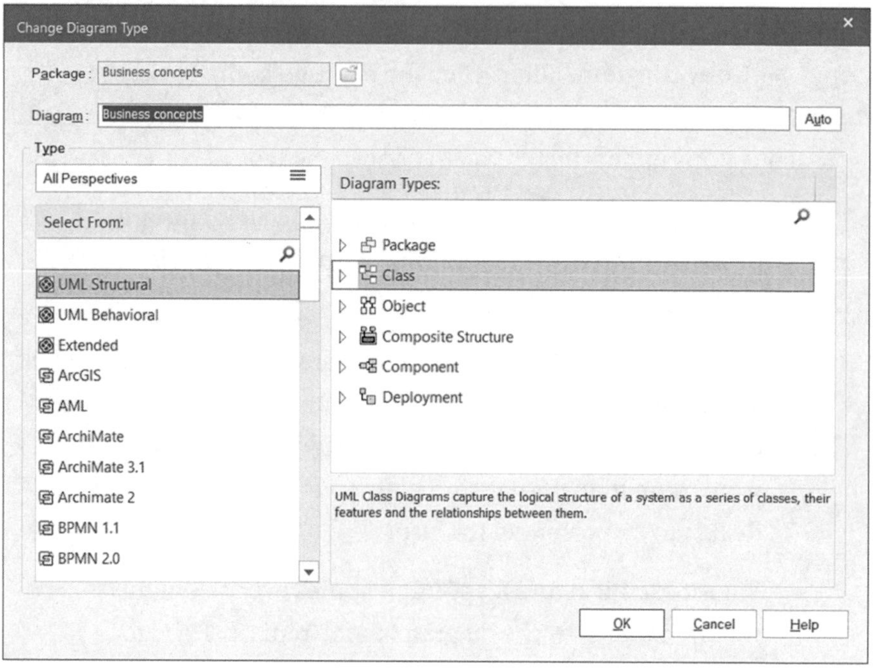

Figure 5-6. *Change diagram type*

Status Colors

Some elements, like "Requirements," have a status that is important to them. For requirements, this could be an indication where in their lifecycle they are. Are they just "proposed" by the analyst or "validated" by business? Already "implemented"?

Therefore, the "Requirements" stereotype allows to show a status color on diagrams, so that you can easily see what status they are in.

Suppose we use the "Requirements" type to model the business plans as part of the Enterprise Architecture. Remember Systemplar has some business initiatives where a new system, called Origa, must be implemented for partner management. We could decompose the requirements as shown in Figure 5-7.

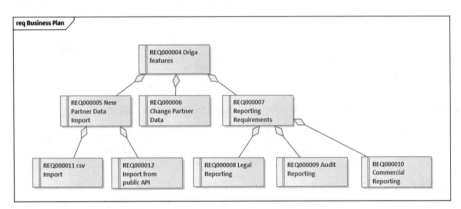

Figure 5-7. *Business plan for Origa implementation*

Some of these requirements are already validated by business, and one is even already implemented by the software team. With a few simple clicks, we can show that:

- In the properties of the requirements, change the status to the correct one (default = "proposed").

- Go to the Ribbon "Start" ➤ "Preferences" ➤ "Preferences" ➤ "Objects" and check "Use Status Colors on Diagrams."

The result is a visual way of representing the requirements statuses, where yellow means "Proposed," green is "Validated," and gray "Implemented" (Figure 5-8). There are more statuses available, and you can also define your own, as we will see in Chapter 8.

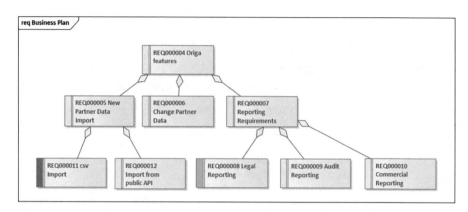

Figure 5-8. *Business plan for Origa implementation with status colors*

Legends

A next step to improve the readability of diagrams is to put a legend on it. To create a legend, just search for the "legend" stereotype in the Toolbox: it is in the "Common Elements" toolbox.

In the dialog box that appears, you can specify the different types of elements and their colors (Figure 5-9).

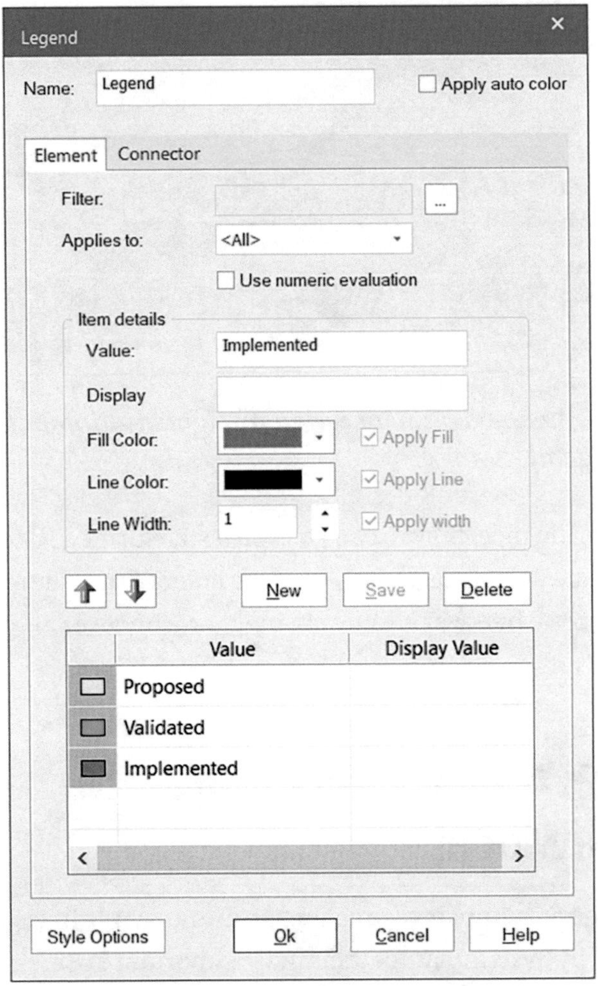

Figure 5-9. *Creating a diagram legend*

The interface to do this is a bit clumsy, since you have to click "New," create the item, and click "Save" without any protection from overriding an already existing element. The result is a nicer diagram that should be self-explanatory (Figure 5-10).

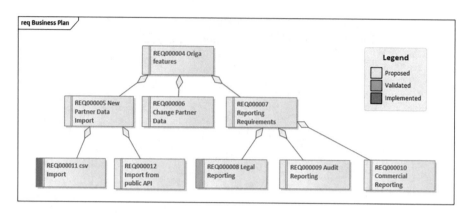

Figure 5-10. *Business plan for Origa implementation with status colors and legend*

This is already nice, but we can go even a step further. We can use legends to create active diagrams where the color of the element on the diagram changes whenever a value changes, or whenever another legend is applied.

Case 5-2: A Heat Map for the Software Model

Let's turn to the Systemplar case again. We are currently investigating the software used by Systemplar for their most important business processes: delivering goods and services to their customers.

Systemplar has historically chosen for a "best of breed" approach to software, especially concerning the service and product delivery. That means a lot of different software, some of them "commercial-off-the-shelf" (COTS) and some of them their own IP (Intellectual Property). There are two more properties relevant: the functional fit and the technical fit of these applications.

We made a simple .csv list of applications we have encountered so far, and their properties. We imported this list into Enterprise Architect.

We then added a diagram with all applications on it, used autolayout to show a simple box layout, and added three legends: one for functional fit, one for technical fit, and one for ownership. Depending on the legend that is active, we can now simply show the "heat map" of the application landscape. Here is the heat map showing the ownership (Figure 5-11).

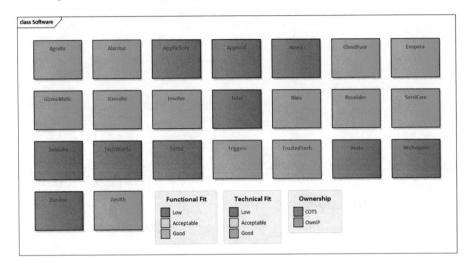

Figure 5-11.   *Heat map of the application landscape*

Curious how we accomplished this? Let's explore the steps.

Step 1: Importing the Data

First, create a package "software" in the "Business concepts" package. Also, create a class and add three tagged values to it by clicking the "New" button (white with yellow star): FunctionalFit, TechnicalFit, and Ownership (Figure 5-12). Don't worry too much about these tagged values – we will discuss them in more detail in Chapter 8. We just need them to store custom information.

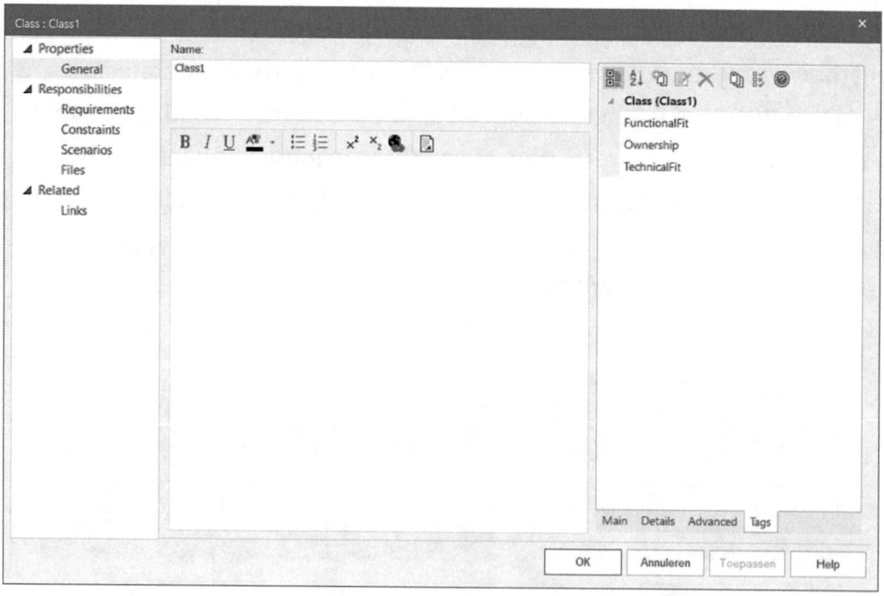

Figure 5-12. *Adding tagged values*

Then we create an import specification "software import" with Type and Name as basic columns and all three tagged values (Figure 5-13).

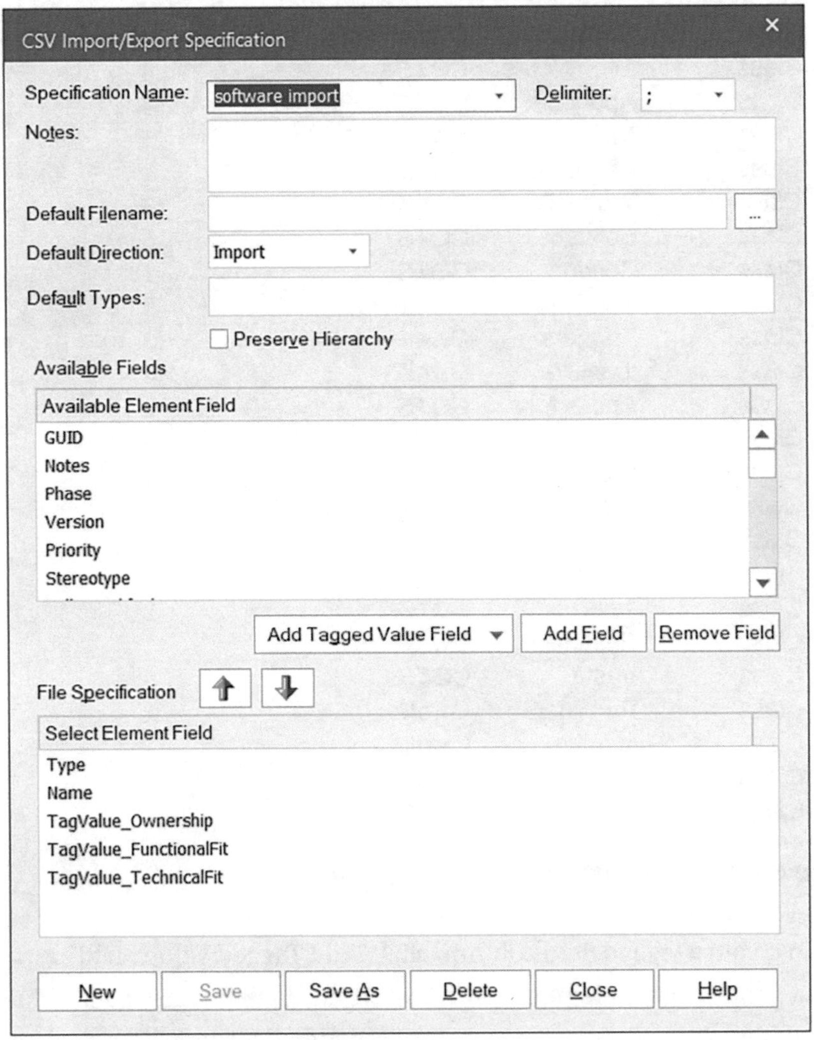

CSV Import/Export Specification ✕

Specification Name: [software import ▾] Delimiter: [; ▾]

Notes: [   ]

Default Filename: [   ] [...]

Default Direction: [Import ▾]

Default Types: [   ]

☐ Preserve Hierarchy

Available Fields

Available Element Field
GUID
Notes
Phase
Version
Priority
Stereotype

[Add Tagged Value Field ▾] [Add Field] [Remove Field]

File Specification [⬆] [⬇]

Select Element Field
Type
Name
TagValue_Ownership
TagValue_FunctionalFit
TagValue_TechnicalFit

[New] [Save] [Save As] [Delete] [Close] [Help]

Figure 5-13. *CSV import specification*

This is the software list as a spreadsheet (Figure 5-14).

	A	B	C	D	E
1	Type	Software	Ownership	Functional F▸	Technical Fit
2	Class	TechWorks	COTS	4	3
3	Class	Appnod	COTS	4	4
4	Class	Nixis	OwnIP	1	2
5	Class	GizmoMatic	OwnIP	1	4
6	Class	TrustedTech	OwnIP	3	3
7	Class	Solalabs	COTS	3	3
8	Class	Zendon	COTS	1	2
9	Class	ServiCare	OwnIP	5	4
10	Class	Triggers	OwnIP	3	4
11	Class	Iconsite	OwnIP	4	4
12	Class	Appfactory	COTS	2	3
13	Class	Avera	COTS	3	4
14	Class	Webvigant	COTS	1	3
15	Class	CloudFuse	OwnIP	4	4
16	Class	Alacrisa	OwnIP	1	5
17	Class	Zenith	OwnIP	1	2
18	Class	Jotel	COTS	2	4
19	Class	Enspera	OwnIP	1	2
20	Class	Vesta	COTS	3	4
21	Class	Proviider	OwnIP	1	3
22	Class	Insolve	OwnIP	1	3
23	Class	Agrello	OwnIP	4	2
24	Class	Tertal	COTS	2	3

Figure 5-14. *The software list as a csv file*

To create a tagged field column, click "Add Tagged Value Field" ➤ "Value," then "Other element." Look for the class where the tagged values were added. Add all three: Ownership, Functional Fit, and Technical Fit (Figure 5-15).

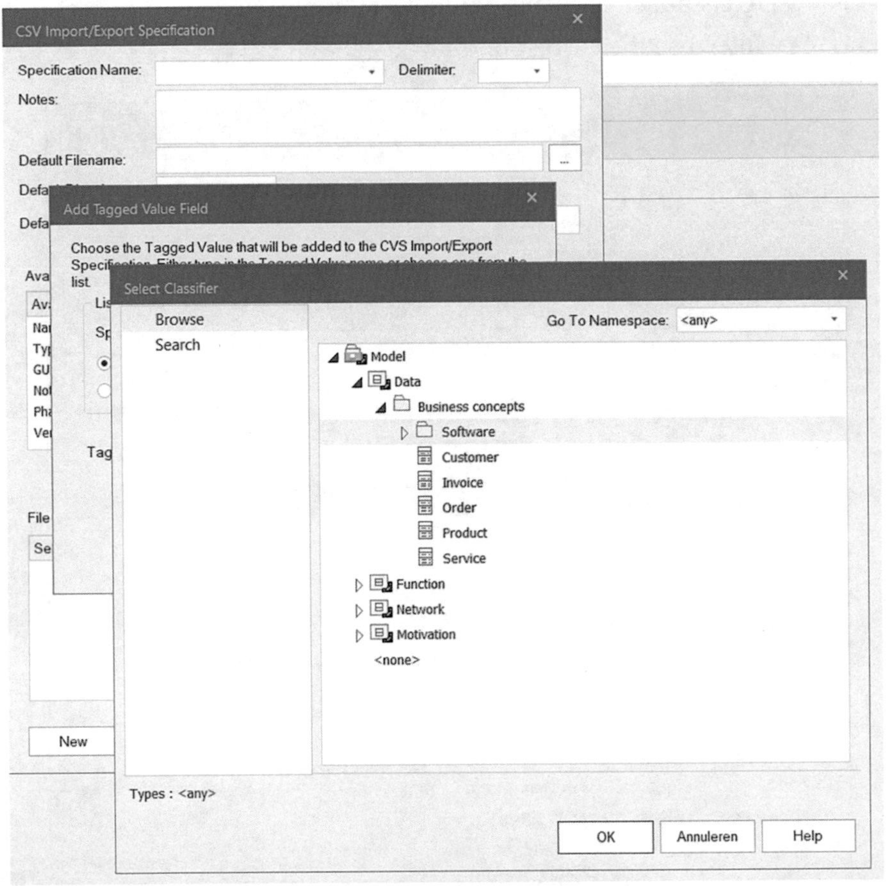

Figure 5-15. *Adding a tagged field column*

Once this import specification is ready, importing the list only takes seconds (Figure 5-16).

Step 2: Creating the Legends

Now we can add a diagram, add the software applications to it, and use autolayout. Then we create three legends: one for ownership, one for FunctionalFit, and one for TechnicalFit.

For each legend, check "Apply auto color" in the legend properties (top right). As a filter, use the corresponding tagged value.

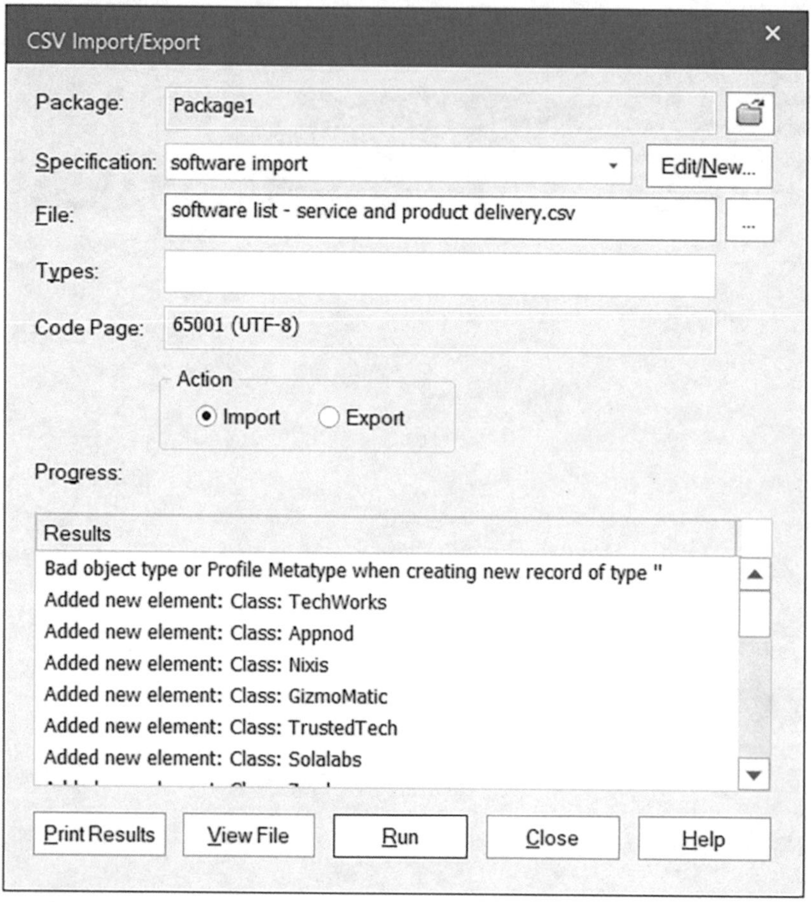

Figure 5-16. *Importing the software list*

The "ownership" and "functional fit" legends look like Figure 5-17 (the "technical fit" legend is almost identical to the "functional fit" one).

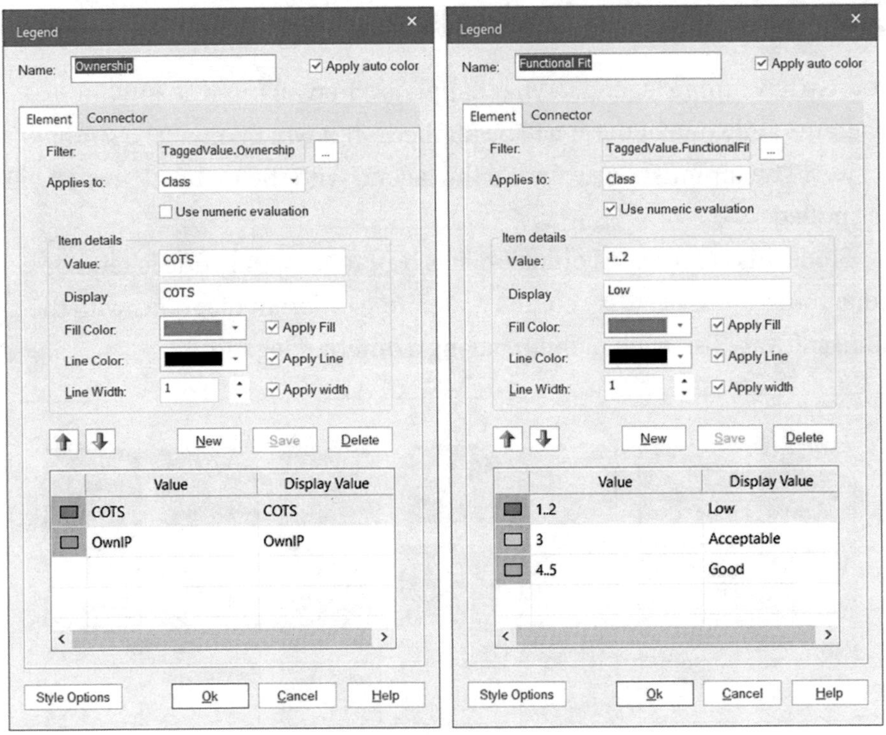

Figure 5-17. *Ownership and functional fit legends*

As you can see, the top parts of these legends are identical. The difference is that functional fit is a numerical field, so we check "Use numeric evaluation." Then we apply ranges: 1..2 means that the element will be marked in red with legend description "Low," 3 will be colored yellow with legend description "Acceptable," and 4..5 is green with description "Good" (Figure 5-18).

Compared to that, the ownership legend is simpler: if the tagged value is "COTS," we display "COTS," and if it is "OwnIP," we display "OwnIP" (of course, we could change the legend value, but for now we keep them equal).

Step 3: Using the Legends

Now we have three legends. What happens when all three are on the diagram? Only one of them will be applied – but which one? The simple answer: The topmost one wins. So the legend with the highest Z-order will be applied.

Since this can create confusion, it is best to have only one legend on a diagram. In this case, we could create three different diagrams with the same software list, each of them having a different legend.

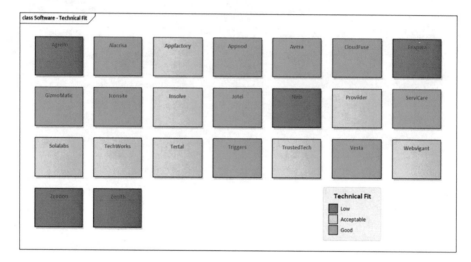

Figure 5-18. *Technical fit "heat map"*

A diagram like the technical fit diagram is called a "heat map" because it quickly shows where the burning issues are. Managers love heat maps, because they provide overview and make complex things easier to manage. Good to know that Enterprise Architect supports heat maps in a neat way!

Adding Elements to the Same Diagram Twice

Sometimes, you want to add the same element to a diagram twice. For example, when there are lots of connectors to an element, it would be nice if we could have two instances of that element on the same diagram so we can avoid clutter created by overlapping connectors.

However, when you try to do this, Enterprise Architect says no (Figure 5-19).

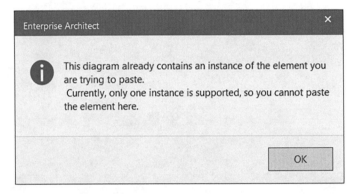

Figure 5-19. *This element is already present on the diagram*

Yet there is a way to circumvent this restriction.

First, set the line style to "Custom Line" by invoking the context menu on the connector and choosing "Line Style" ➤ "Custom."

Then, reopen the context menu and choose "Virtualize connector end" and "Source" or "Target," depending on the direction of the connector. You get a "copy" of the element (Figure 5-20).

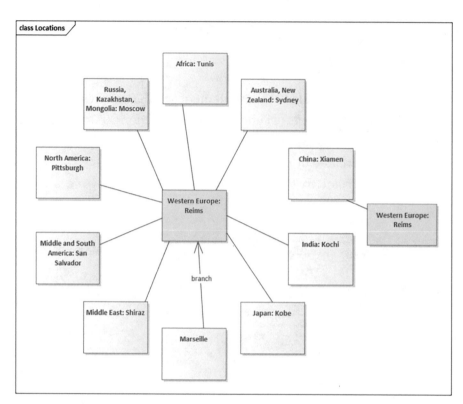

Figure 5-20. *Second instance of an element on a diagram*

This second instance does not behave entirely independently. For instance, if you select one of both "copies," both get selected. That means you cannot give them a different layout such as color or border width. Also, and predictably, if you double-click one of the "copies," you get the properties of the original element. However, you can move them around independently, and that is what counts.

You can undo this by opening the context menu on the connector and removing the checkmark before the virtualized connector end.

Note   Use this tip sparingly, because it can cause confusion – people might think there are two different "headquarters" in Reims!

Showing Alternative Info and Notes

Most elements can have attributes, which you can use to store extra information about the element. Attributes can even have notes, and the good news is that you can show these as a "linked note" on a diagram.

Suppose we want to indicate that Reims is the headquarter office of Systemplar and what that means.

As a first step, we add an attribute "status" with value "headquarters" to the Reims class. Right-click the Reims element, and choose "Features" ➤ "Attributes." Fill out the fields Attribute ("status") and Initial Value ("headquarters"). Then add a note text "Reims is the main office where most of the internal processes are centralized."

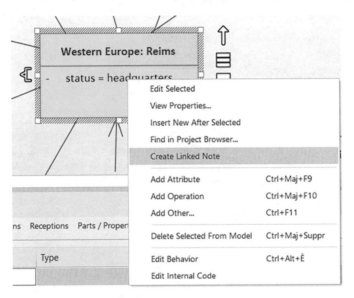

Figure 5-21. *Adding an attribute*

Now we will add the note to our diagram. Select the attribute of the Reims element, and from the context menu, choose "Create Linked Note" (Figures 5-21 and 5-22).

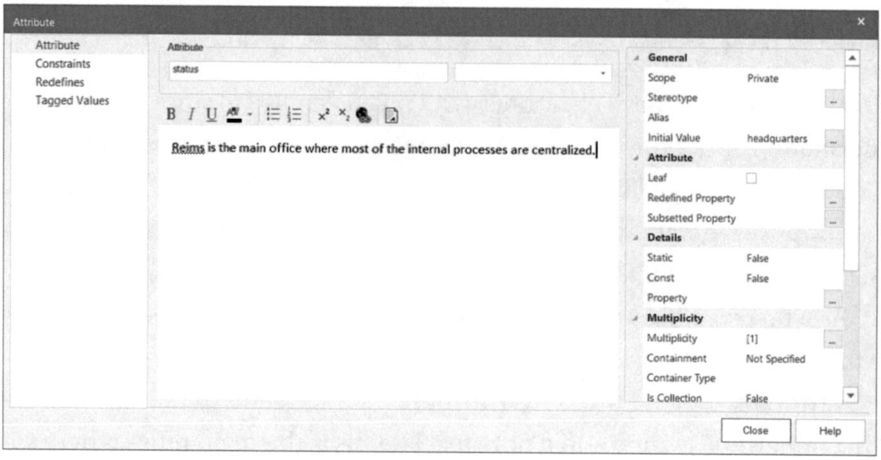

Figure 5-22. *Creating a linked note*

The diagram then looks like Figure 5-23.

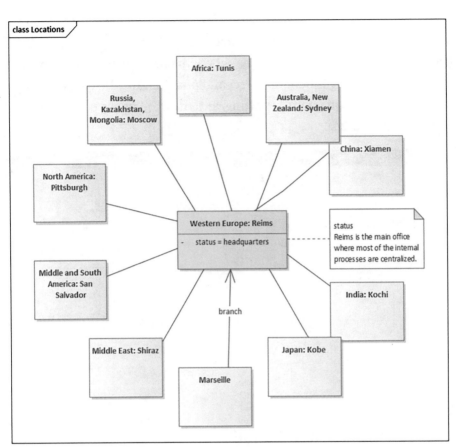

Figure 5-23. *A linked note on a diagram*

Thoughtfully inserting information like this makes a diagram "self-explanatory."

Filtering Diagrams

A useful tool to hide information from a diagram depending on the status of elements is diagram filtering. Remember the business plan with the high-level features for the Origa software that Systemplar is currently developing?

We could make this diagram a lot more active by using a filter based on the phase property of the requirements. Let's assume Systemplar will develop the software in three phases, where the first phase contains a basic import and reporting function, the second phase allows the user to change partner data and some more reporting, and the third phase contains all features (Figure 5-24).

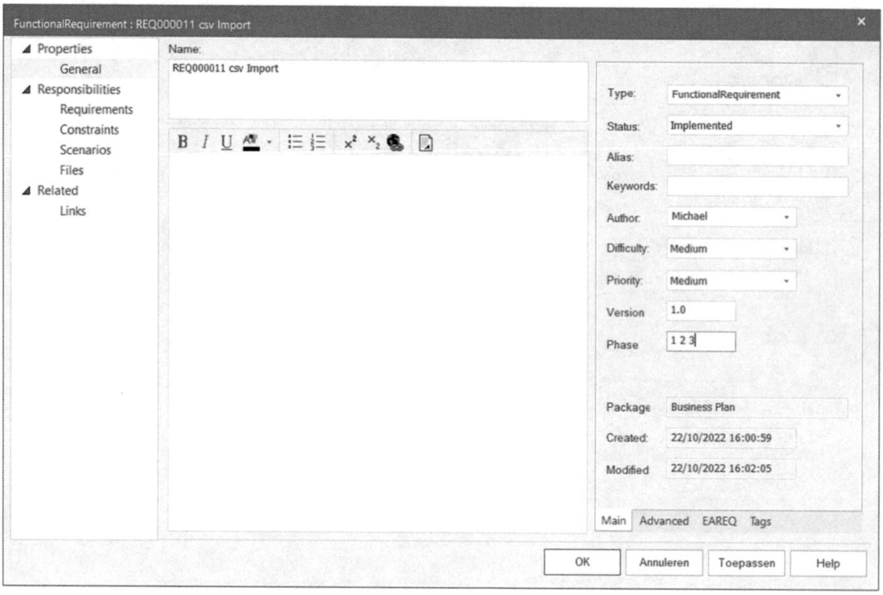

Figure 5-24.   *Adding phase information to an element*

First, fill in the phase property for all phase 1 requirements (REQ00001 and REQ000008). Since they will be realized in phase 1 and continue to function in phases 2 and 3, we fill in "1 2 3" as their phase.

Second, we add "2 3" to the requirements that are planned for phase 2. Lastly, we add "3" for all remaining requirements, including the higher-level requirements REQ000004, REQ000005, and REQ000007.

Now we can use the phase information in a filter (Figure 5-25). Open the Filters & Layers window (Ribbon: "Layout" ➤ "Filters & Layers"). Then add a new filter by clicking the "New" button in the Filters & Layers window. Name the filter "Phase 1." A new dialog shows. Check "Phase" and give it value "1." Do the same for filters "Phase 2" and "Phase 3."

Filter			✕
Active Filter Set:			
Element	▾		
Add Filt...	Field: ▲	Condition	Value
☐	Filename	Contains	*<Search Term>*
☐	GenType	Contains	*<Search Term>*
☐	Keywords	Contains	*<Search Term>*
☐	Matches View	Equal To	True
☐	Name	Contains	*<Search Term>*
☐	Notes	Contains	*<Search Term>*
☐	ObjectType	Contains	*<Search Term>*
☑	Phase	Contains	1
☐	Printable	Equal To	True
☐	Priority	Contains	*<Search Term>*
☐	RequirementType	Contains	*<Search Term>*
Check All	Uncheck All		OK Cancel Help

Figure 5-25. *Defining a filter for phase 1*

Now that the filters are defined, we can use them. Just check the box before the filter, and the diagram will show the corresponding requirements in full color, graying out the requirements for other phases (Figure 5-26).

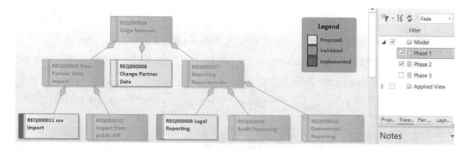

Figure 5-26. *Applying diagram filters for phases 1 and 2*

Instead of graying out the requirements for other phases, you can also hide them or select the relevant ones. Good to know if you want to create a diagram containing only the requirements for phase 1, for example.

Different Views: List, Gantt, Specification, and More

Depending on your purpose, some information is easier to work with if it is presented in another way than the usual diagram where every element has a full-blown visual representation.

The Specification Manager

In our example, the business analyst that is working on the Origa business plan probably wants a more "word processing"–like view on the requirements list. To view the requirements like this, go to the Ribbon and click "Design" ➤ "Specification View" (Figure 5-27).

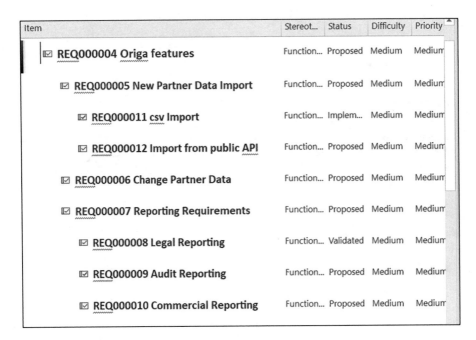

Figure 5-27. *The Specification Manager*

As you can see, the Specification Manager reflects the structure of the requirements as they show up in the Project Browser. You can change this structure by simply dragging the requirements to their correct parent in the Project Browser.

From the Specification Manager, you can add, delete, and change the requirements.

A List View

Another powerful way of representing information on a diagram is the list view. In the Ribbon, click "Design" ➤ "List View" to get all elements on a simple list (Figure 5-28).

Then you can group by any column, for example, status, by dragging the column name to the bar above it.

Status			
▼ Name	▼ Status	▼ Type	▼ Modified ▼
◢ **Status: Implemented**			
☑ REQ000011 csv Import	Implemented	Requirement	28/10/2022
◢ **Status: Proposed**			
☑ REQ000005 New Partner Data Import	Proposed	Requirement	28/10/2022
☑ REQ000004 Origa features	Proposed	Requirement	28/10/2022
☑ REQ000003: Replace IDALGO product line	Proposed	Requirement	28/10/2022
☑ REQ000012 Import from public API	Proposed	Requirement	28/10/2022
☑ REQ000006 Change Partner Data	Proposed	Requirement	28/10/2022
☑ REQ000007 Reporting Requirements	Proposed	Requirement	28/10/2022
☑ REQ000010 Commercial Reporting	Proposed	Requirement	28/10/2022
☑ REQ000009 Audit Reporting	Proposed	Requirement	28/10/2022
▤	Proposed	Text	22/10/2022
◢ **Status: Validated**			
☑ REQ000008 Legal Reporting	Validated	Requirement	28/10/2022

Figure 5-28. *List view*

This is also useful if you want to export the data to a spreadsheet application (or any other software, for that matter).

Just select the rows you want to export, press Ctrl+C, and turn to the spreadsheet application, where Ctrl+V does the trick. This even allows you to export a random set of elements, instead of having to put them together under the same package.

A Gantt Chart

The last "special view" we discuss here is the Gantt chart view. In the Ribbon, select "Design" ➤ "Gantt View" to activate this view (Figure 5-29).

Before the actual Gantt chart becomes available, you have to add resources to the elements. Right-click an element and choose "Add Resources...." Fill out the name, role, begin date, and end date for all relevant elements, and you get a view like Figure 5-29.

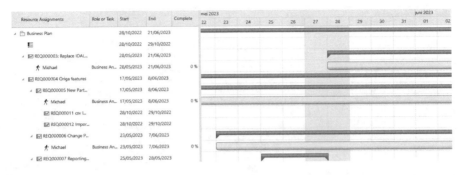

Figure 5-29. *A Gantt chart*

You can export this diagram to an image file, for example, to impress inexperienced people with your project management skills. Right-click the Gantt chart and choose "Save Image to File..." for this.

Special Diagrams

Some diagrams don't contain regular modeling content, yet they are useful to serve as a jump board or to show quantitative information about some aspect of the model.

Navigation Cells

A diagram that contains navigation cells helps users (consumers of information) find their way in a complicated model with lots of different diagrams.

Adding navigation cells is easy: just drag a diagram from the Project Browser to an empty space on the navigation cell diagram, and choose "Navigation cell" in the dialog that appears. The next dialog allows you to select a graphic, and the navigation cell appears on the diagram.

A typical diagram with navigation cells looks like Figure 5-30.

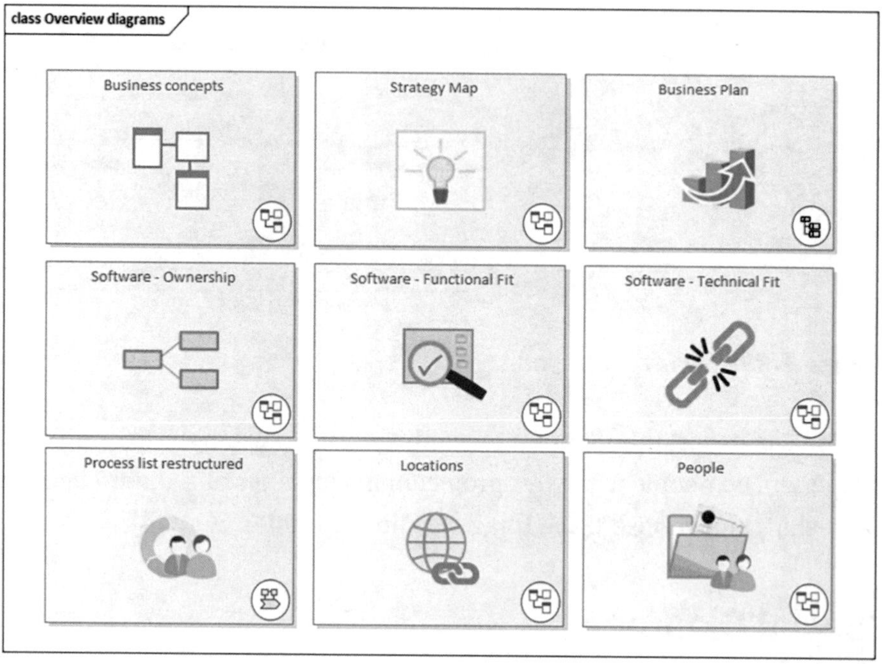

Figure 5-30. *A navigation cell diagram*

By clicking a navigation cell, you end up in the corresponding diagram. This is especially useful if you create a website from the model, and if you use these navigation cell diagrams as a model default (see further in this chapter).

The other options beside "Navigation Cell" are equally interesting:

- Diagram frame: A frame containing the contents of the diagram.

- Diagram reference: An empty frame.

- Hyperlink: A simple hyperlink. Useful if there is not a lot of space available.

- List: A list containing the elements of the diagram. The dialog that pops up shows the SQL statement that generates this list. If you are handy with SQL and you know the Enterprise Architect data model, you can easily modify this query to adapt it to your needs.

Package Contents

A diagram can also contain a reference to a package instead of another diagram. If you drag a package from the Project Browser to a diagram, a context menu pops up. Choose "Package element" to show the contents of a package as a list on the diagram. Another view with a query behind it is created when you select "Package as list" (Figure 5-31).

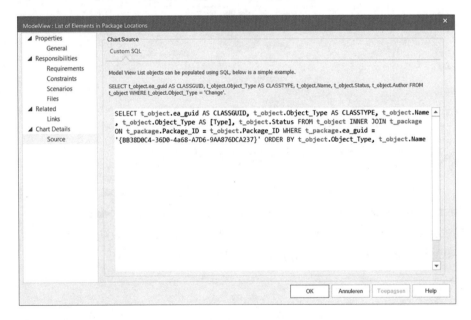

Figure 5-31. *Package as list*

If this list is longer than what the frame allows to show, the frame will indicate how many elements are shown and the total number of elements. Just make the frame longer to show more.

Graphs

A last useful representation is graphs. As an example, we can show the contents of the business plan package containing the requirements for the two big projects as a pie chart, based on their status (Figure 5-32).

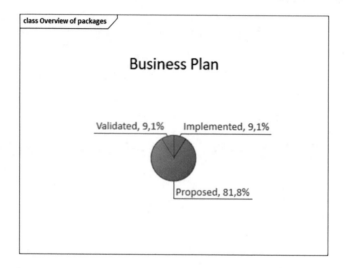

Figure 5-32. *The business plan as a pie chart*

Instead of a pie chart, you can also choose a 2D or 3D bar chart or a "heat map" where you can even show two properties in a visual way.

Besides that, you can work with external data (from csv) instead of using package data from Enterprise Architect (Figure 5-33).

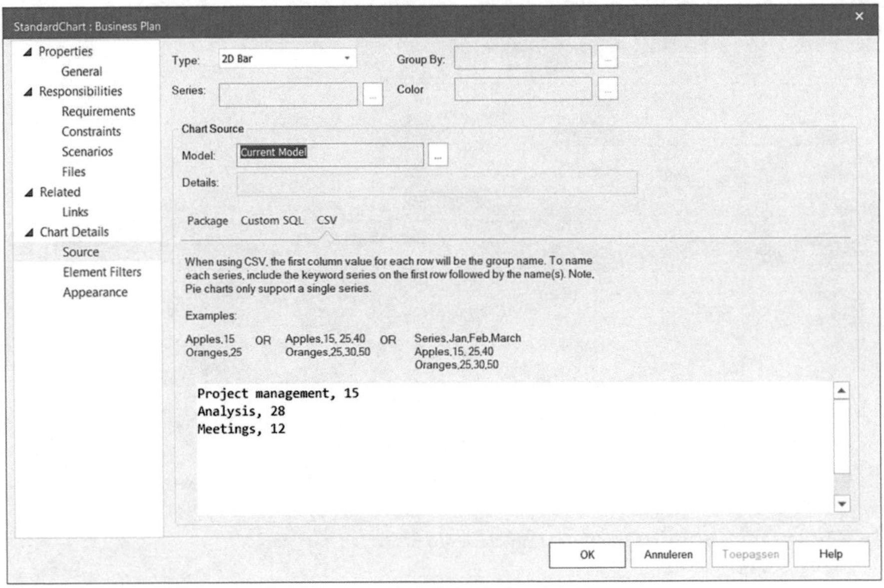

Figure 5-33. *Working with external data in charts*

Saving Time Opening the Right Diagrams

If you work with Enterprise Architect regularly, you'll find yourself navigating through the Project Browser every time, looking for the same diagrams again and again. Here are some ways to save time and frustration.

User and Model Default

The navigation cell diagram becomes especially useful if you combine it with this nifty little trick: you can specify which diagram should be active when you open the model. Typically, an overview diagram is used for that so that you have one-click access to the most important diagrams.

Setting the current diagram as a default is easy: go to the Ribbon, click "Start" ➤ "Default Diagram" ➤ "Set Current as Default." Depending on your version of Enterprise Architect, you can set this default for yourself (user default) or for everyone (model default – Figure 5-34).

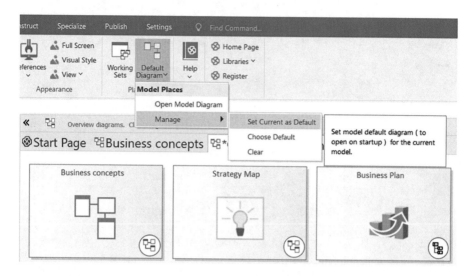

Figure 5-34. *Set current diagram as model default*

Working Sets

An even more flexible way to have your most used diagrams at hand is by defining working sets. Create a working set by going to the Ribbon. Choose "Start" ➤ "Working Sets." Then right-click in the working sets window and choose "Add Working Set." The dialog that appears lets you include open windows, but also others, to the new working set (Figure 5-35).

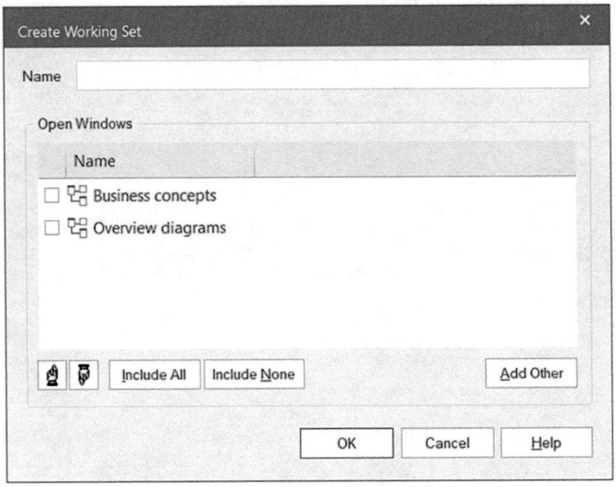

Figure 5-35. *Create a working set*

You can not only add diagrams to the Working Sets but also searches, matrices, and other stuff you want to quickly access.

Save As a Shortcut

A last way to save time opening the right diagrams relies on shortcuts. Go to the start button (top left) and choose "Save as a Shortcut." Then fill out the dialog window that appears (Figure 5-36).

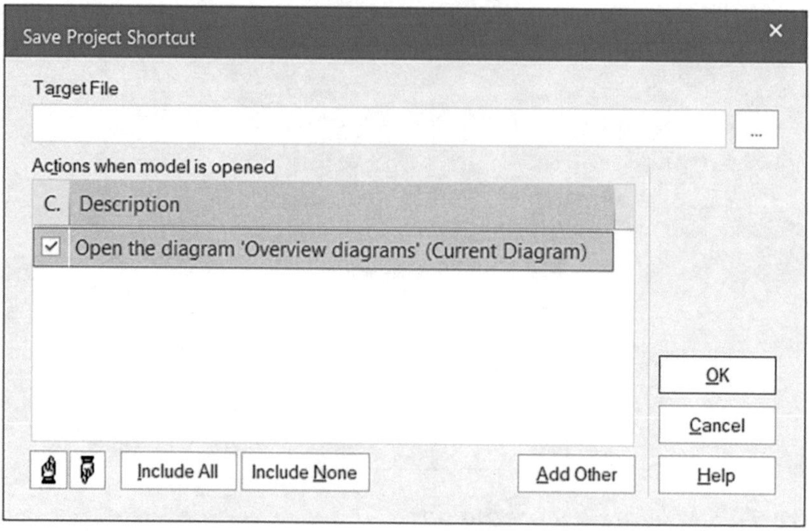

Figure 5-36. *Save as a shortcut*

You can add multiple shortcuts to the same project, each with different settings. For example, if you work on the project as a project manager and as an architect, you probably need different diagrams depending on your role that day.

Importing Graphics

Some diagrams are much easier to understand if you import external graphic elements to them. A good example is the list of locations: it makes sense to show these on a world map with their approximate location.

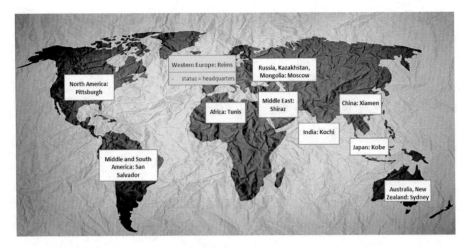

Figure 5-37. *Map of the world*

Importing a map like this is simple: drag it from a system folder to an empty space on the diagram (Figure 5-37). A dialog box pops up, allowing you to choose:

- Hyperlink (open/edit): Do not insert the image itself, only a link to the file so you can open or edit it.

- Artifact (internal/external): Add the image as an element, either stored internally or just as a linked artifact.

- Image asset: Add the image to the Enterprise Architect database and show it on the diagram as a graphic, showing its name at the bottom.

- Insert: Add the image but do not show its name.

Diagram-Related Preferences

Like with connectors and elements, Enterprise Architect has a series of settings that influence how a diagram looks.

Some of these settings sit with the diagram properties (right-click – "Properties"):

- Diagram – Use Alias if available: Instead of showing the name of the element, show the alias if it is not empty. Useful if you work with abbreviations or multiple languages, so you can easily switch between languages.

- Diagram – Disable fully scoped object names: Do not show the parent of the element as a prefix to the element name. Can help to make diagrams simpler and visually less cluttered.

- Elements – Hand Drawn: Make the elements appear if they were drawn by hand. Conveys the message "This is work in progress – please give feedback."

- Elements – Whiteboard Mode: Show no colors. Can be combined with hand drawn mode to actually look like it has been drawn on a whiteboard.

- Connectors – Show Relationships: By unchecking this, all connectors on the current diagram will be hidden.

- Theme: Apply a different theme to the diagram than the one that is globally used. This applies to fonts, colors, line thickness, the gradient color, a background image, and the element shadowing.

Other diagram options can be found in the general settings ("Start" ➤ "Preferences" ➤ "Diagram"):

- Enable connector jumps: If two connectors cross, have one of them show an arc so you know them separate.

- Themes: Apply a globally used theme.

- Gradients and background: Set the default gradient and background.

- Standard colors: Set the default colors for elements, notes, and connectors, for example, to reflect the corporate style.

- Appearance: Here, you can choose to apply shadows to elements and connectors and the "hand drawn" font that is used. You can also specify a watermark that is applied to diagrams.

- Behavior: The default setting is that diagrams, unlike elements and connectors, are not automatically saved. Here, you can choose to automatically save changes to diagrams.

Summary

In this chapter, we covered quite some tips to work with diagrams. We showed how to lay out them, how to reveal or hide information on diagrams, and what different types of diagrams there are. As an extra, we discussed ways to save time by creating working sets and making shortcuts to the model. The next chapter will give even more information about "working" in Enterprise Architect and especially about working in an efficient way.

CHAPTER 6

Different Ways of Handling "Work to Do"

With the Systemplar Enterprise Architecture Model (SEAM) growing, we start to feel the need to keep a list of "work in progress" (WIP). There are different alternatives. Maybe simply bookmarking elements would suffice? Or tagging work in progress with a #todo tag? A bit more elaborate is to use Kanban diagrams. Still more elaborate are Enterprise Architect's Project Management features. Let's explore the pros and cons of each of these solutions.

Bookmarking Elements

Any Enterprise Architect element, including notes, can bear a bookmark. An inverted red triangle on top of the element visualizes this bookmark, as shown in Figure 6-1.

© Peter Doomen 2023
P. Doomen, *Introduction to SparxSystems Enterprise Architect,*
https://doi.org/10.1007/978-1-4842-9312-6_6

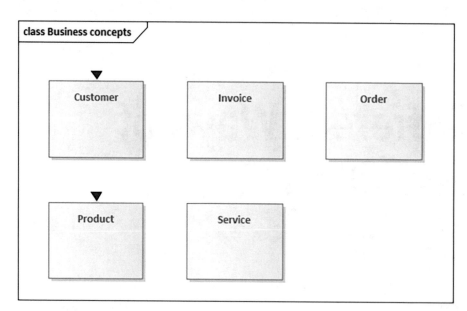

Figure 6-1. *Bookmarked elements*

You can add or remove a bookmark from an element by selecting it and pressing Ctrl+Shift. This also works if multiple elements have been selected.

Now what if you want to have an overview of all elements that have a bookmark? Do you have to open diagrams one by one to visually inspect them?

Of course not. There is a well-hidden search option that you can activate by pressing Ctrl+F and choosing "Diagram Searches" ➤ "Find Bookmarked Elements." Then click the green arrow button, as shown in Figure 6-2.

Object	Type	Stereotype	Scope	Status	Phase
Marketing process	Activity	process	Public	Proposed	1.0
Procurement process	Activity	process	Public	Proposed	1.0
Sales process	Activity	process	Public	Proposed	1.0
Customer	Class		Public	Proposed	1.0
Product	Class		Public	Proposed	1.0
	Note		Public	Proposed	1.0

Figure 6-2. *Finding bookmarked elements*

While this works and is easy to do, there are a few important disadvantages to using this approach:

- The bookmark does not tell you what the status of an element is, apart from the fact that "work needs to be done." Is it actually taken up by someone? What's the progress? Is it waiting on input from someone else?

- It only tells you that "some" work has to be done at a general element level. Do you still need to work on the description? Links to other elements? Trying to figure out the importance or priority of an element?

Adding #todo to Elements

By adding a simple #todo tag to the description of an element, you can alleviate the disadvantages of simple bookmarks to a certain extent. For example, it allows you to specify what work still needs to be done and who is going to take it up.

Searching for #todos is a matter of using a simple search for "#todo" in the Find in Project window. Press Ctrl+F to activate it, then add #todo in the "Search Theme" field, and select "Common Searches" ➤ "Simple." Click the green arrow button to launch the search, as shown in Figure 6-3.

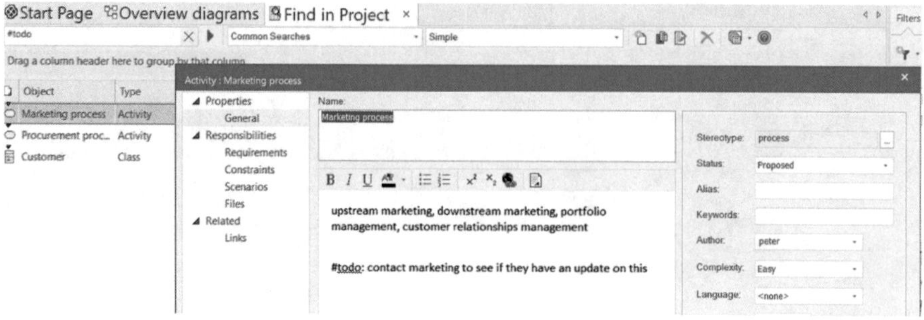

Figure 6-3. *Find in Project*

A disadvantage of this system is that you don't have an actual status overview of the work in progress. It merely shows a list of items to work on. Can we overcome this? Sure!

Using Swimlanes to Get a Status Overview

Before the creative product developers at SparxSystems came up with the special Kanban feature, we could rely on the general "swimlanes" functionality to mimic a Kanban diagram.

Right-click a diagram and choose "Swimlanes and Matrix." Then specify a name and a color for each lane. Figure 6-4 illustrates this.

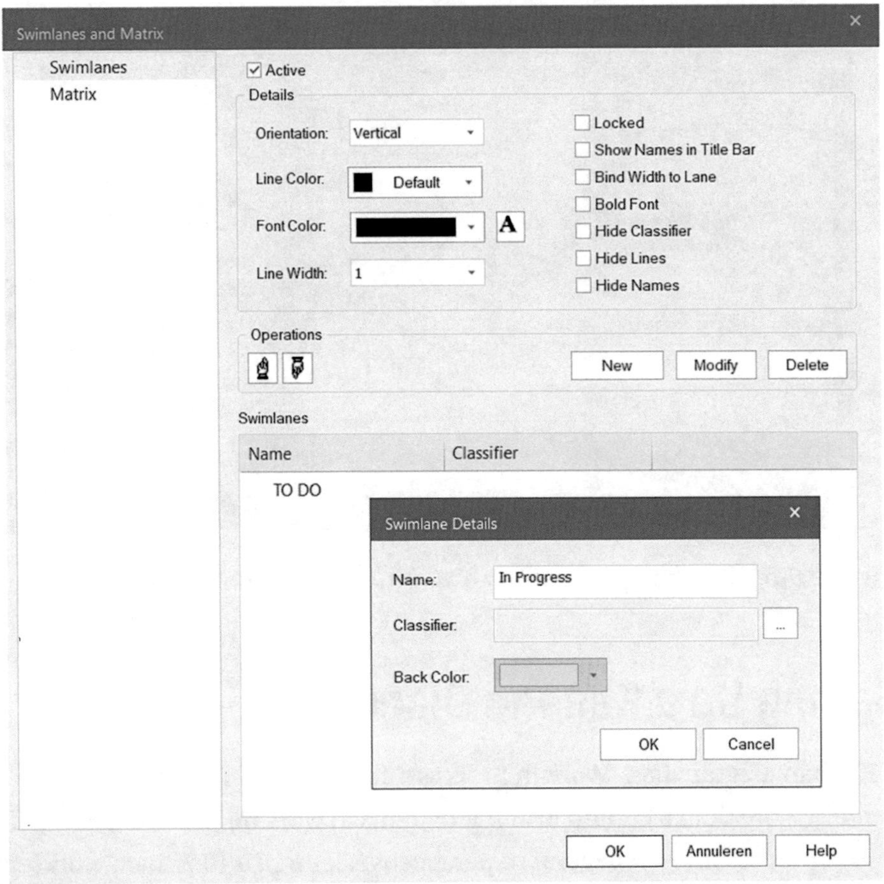

Figure 6-4. *Swimlanes definition*

Then you simply drag all elements that are on your to-do list from the Project Browser to the diagram (Figure 6-5). This works, but the Kanban diagram feature offers more functionality, and it is as simple in use.

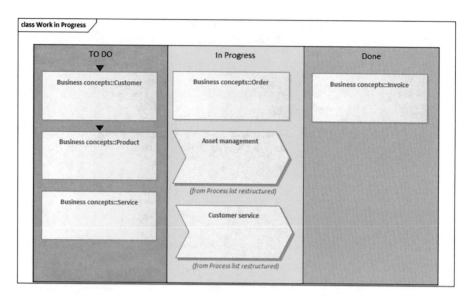

Figure 6-5. *Work in progress as a swimlane diagram*

Setting Up a Kanban Diagram

A Kanban diagram has "Work in Progress" limits: each lane should not contain more than a certain number of items to work on. This makes sense from a process flow management perspective: if there is too much work in progress for the people doing it, the result is that on average, items get finished slower. On the other hand, if there is too little work in progress, the workflow can get stuck too because some items might take longer to finish than expected, for example, because input from a third party is required.

One of the basic ideas of Kanban is to optimize flow by balancing work in progress against the workforce doing the work. Enterprise Architect supports this idea with functionality.

Besides that, the Kanban feature of Enterprise Architect offers more advantages:

- You don't have to specify names for the lanes – the diagram comes preloaded with a standard set (which of course you can change if needed).

- Element fields can be "tied" to the Kanban lane they are in. For example, you could use the Phase field of the elements to indicate their status. If you change their status, they'll change lanes on the board and vice versa.

- Elements in the Kanban list show up as a rectangle, irrespective of their type or stereotype, with an indication of the "author" and a different color and shade per author – an easy way to visualize who is working on what.

Let us dive into the SEAM project and see how we can use a standard Kanban board to get an overview of all the work that needs to be done to document the enterprise architecture of Systemplar.

Case 6-1: A Kanban Diagram for the Enterprise Architecture

Setting Up the First Version

Setting up an initial version of the Kanban diagram is easy: we just create a new diagram of the type "Kanban" – "Basic," as you can see in Figure 6-6.

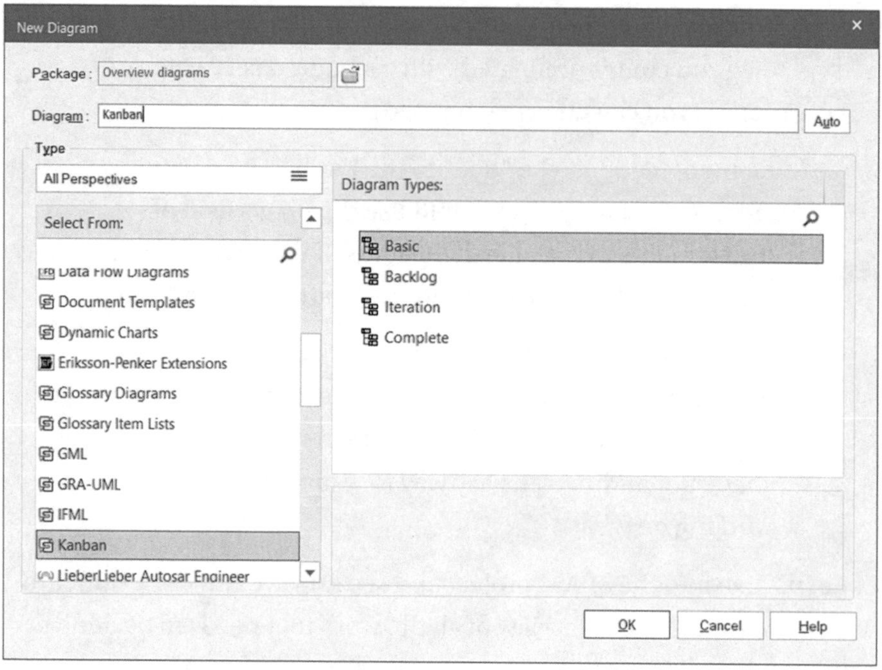

Figure 6-6. *Kanban basic diagram*

This creates a diagram with four swimlanes, called "Backlog," "Queue," "In Progress," and "Done." For now, let's keep this basic structure.

Then we start dragging work from the Project Browser into the diagram. For some items, we change the name of the "author" in the element's properties to reflect who would work on the item. We note that each "author" gets their own color set (Figure 6-7).

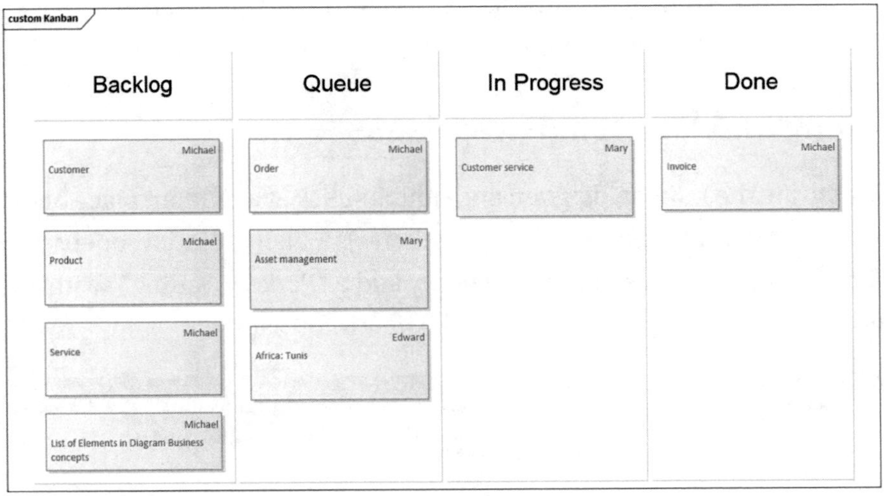

Figure 6-7. A Kanban board with items

Note that the board shows a variety of items: some are processes, others classes, and still others even diagrams. Yet all of them get a standard-width representation in a Kanban board, so that the width of the lanes can be kept equal too.

Adapting the Kanban Diagram

The diagram already gave a good overview of work in progress on the Enterprise Architecture project, but we want more. Specifically, we want to do the following:

- Create an extra column "Parked/waiting," which is a typical status for enterprise architecture work... you are always dependent on somebody else.

- Tie the item status on the board to the "phase" field of the element, so all output we create would reflect the actual status of the items.

- Put "Work in Progress limits" to the "In Progress" lane so that focus can be kept.

Adding and Removing Swimlanes

We activate the Kanban diagram and double-click at a random place on the header (with the names of the swimlanes). A dialog window opens (Figure 6-8). Using this dialog, we simply add a "Parked/waiting" swimlane and close the dialog window, saving the new information.

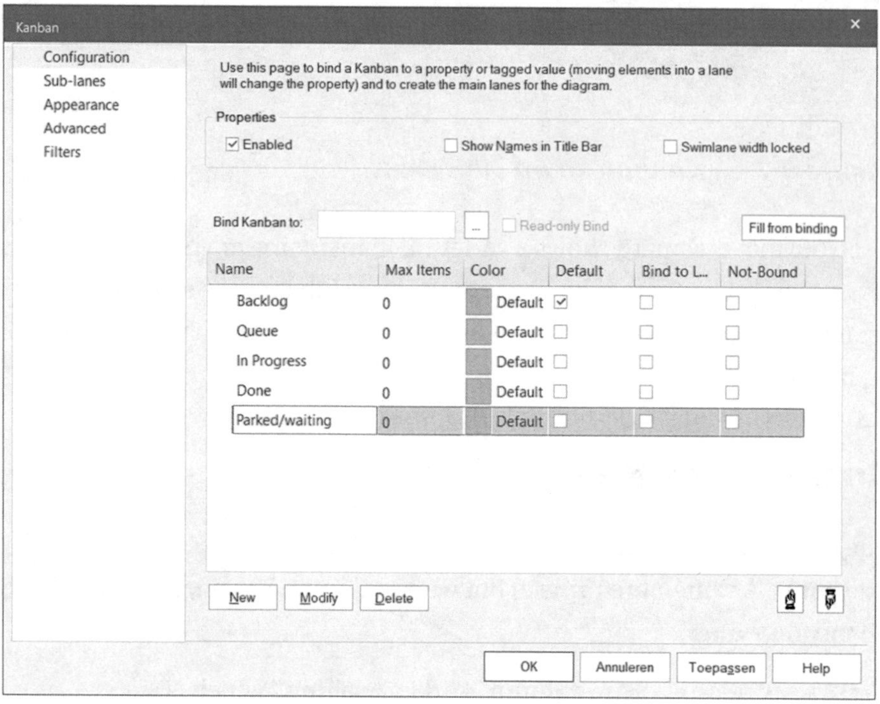

Figure 6-8. *Adding a swimlane*

Tying the Item Status to the Phase Field

Verify the lane actually gets added to the diagram, then reopen the Kanban dialog. There, we choose to bind the Kanban status to the element field "Phase" and check all "Bind to left" boxes, so every swimlane is bound (Figure 6-9).

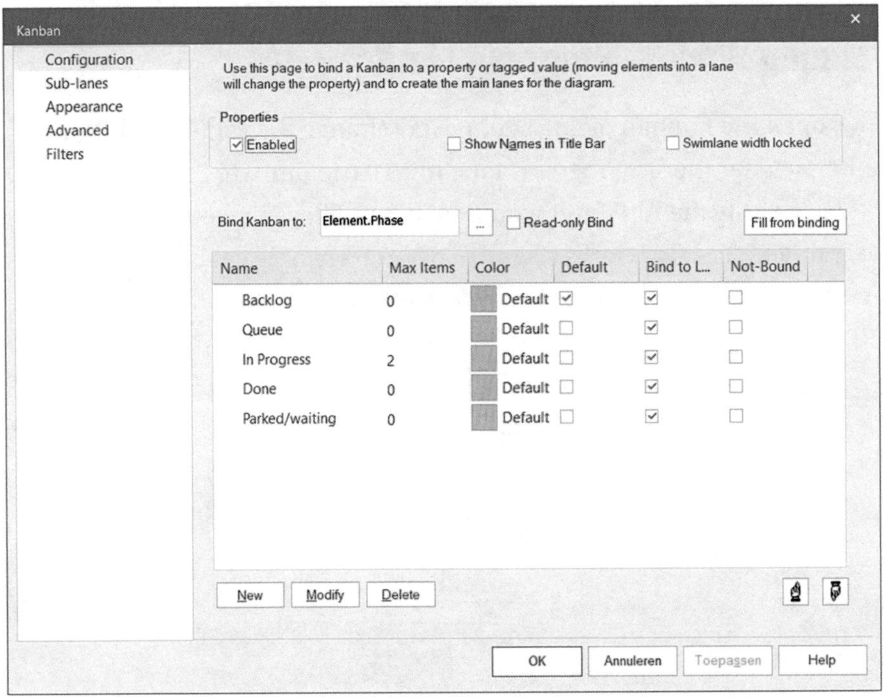

Figure 6-9. *Binding the Kanban status to the phase field*

From now on, the "phase" field of the items on the Kanban board will reflect the name of the swimlane they were in.

Note   When moving items between bound lanes, you have to confirm the move by clicking the "move to" context dialog that pops up. This is confusing at first, but once you are used to it, it is the fastest way of approving the move.

The Kanban dialog has a button called "Fill from binding": if the bound field ("phase") already contains the swimlane names, you can fill up the swimlane names from these values by clicking this button. If you already set up a Kanban board with the appropriate swimlanes, don't touch this button.

Defining Work in Progress Limits

Now, open the Kanban dialog again. Now change the value of the "Max Items" field for the "In Progress" lane from 0 (no limit) to 2.

Then verify the WIP limit would raise a red flag if it would be overridden. This also works (Figure 6-10). The simple yet powerful Kanban method will help you to keep an overview of work in progress, and the nice WIP limit feature helps not to take up too much work at once.

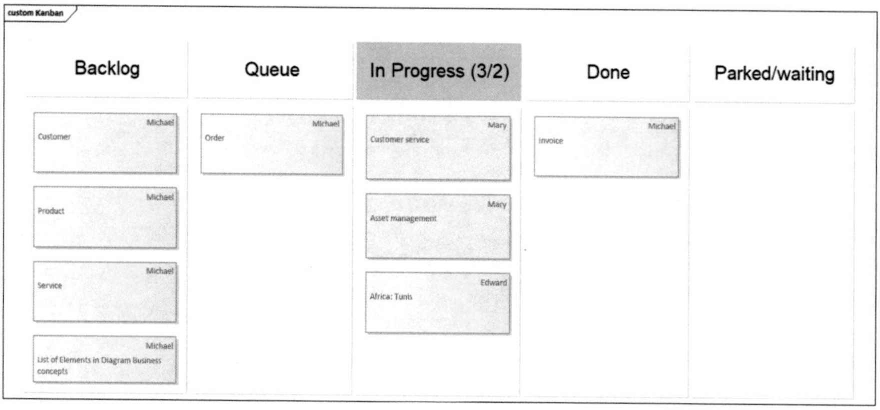

Figure 6-10. *An overrun of the work in progress limit*

Tip   If there are lots of items on the Kanban board, you can apply diagram filters (see the previous chapter) to limit the amount of information you have to process.

Project Management in the EA Model

A final way to keep track of tasks is by using the Project Management feature of Enterprise Architect. This is rather "old-style" project management: a list of tasks to be kept up to date manually and without a link to elements in the model. Nevertheless, if you are looking for a simple project management tool and you are already working with Enterprise Architect, this might be just enough to cover your needs. Go to the Ribbon and choose "Construct" ➤ "Project Management" to get the appropriate dialogs (Figure 6-11).

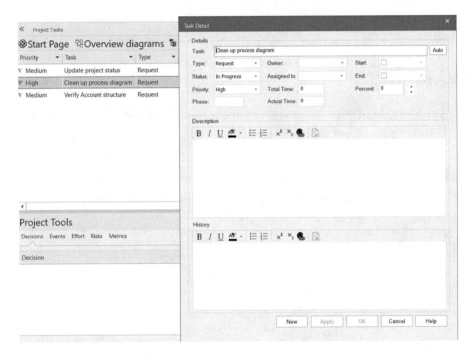

Figure 6-11. *Project management*

Besides tasks, you can keep track of

- Decisions

- Events

- Effort

- Risks

- Metrics

- Issues

These features don't need words to see how to use them, as they are basically simple lists named appropriately.

Summary

This chapter dealt with various ways to organize "work to do" in Enterprise Architect. Especially if multiple people are involved and many tasks are being carried out simultaneously, these features will help to keep an overview and get things done. The next chapter will show different strategies to create output, for example, documents, slideshows, and websites.

CHAPTER 7

Creating Reports and Slideshows

Why does management think EA is an IT issue? Because IT raises the issue and has the skills to build the artifacts that solve it.

—John Zachman

Now that we have imported and structured a lot of information about Systemplar in Enterprise Architect, we can use some of that information to create output for Systemplar employees that do not have access to EA. As always, there are various ways to achieve that target. We will begin with a few simple tricks, gradually creating more refined output and even a full-blown website with every element, connector, and diagram for the Systemplar Enterprise Architecture Model in it.

Diagram Exports

The simplest way to export a diagram is by pasting it to the clipboard.

1. Activate the diagram and press "Ctrl+B," then go to the target such as a slide deck and press "Ctrl+V" (Figure 7-1).

P. Doomen, *Introduction to SparxSystems Enterprise Architect*,
https://doi.org/10.1007/978-1-4842-9312-6_7

2. Note: You can also press "Ctrl+A" to select all diagram elements, then "Ctrl+C" to copy them, but "Ctrl+B" is twice as fast.

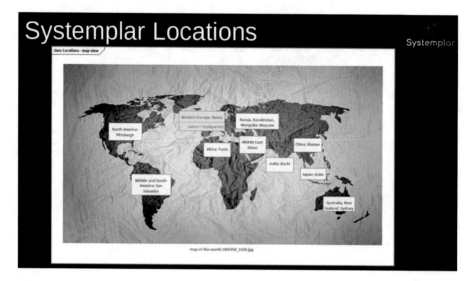

Figure 7-1. *Systemplar locations pasted in a slide deck with Ctrl+B*

If you don't like the border around the image, you can turn this off with "Start" ➤ "Preferences" ➤ "Diagram" and unchecking "Diagram Frames" ➤ "On Clipboard Images."

If you want to export all diagrams in the model or a specific package, you can create a "diagrams-only" document as follows:

1. Select the model root or the package, then go to the Ribbon and click "Publish" ➤ "Report Builder."

2. Choose "Diagram Report" as a template (Figure 7-2). Give the document an appropriate name ("SEAM Diagrams") and click "Generate." After the generation is complete, click "View" to view

the document in the Enterprise Architect internal
document viewer (you can change this by unchecking
the box "Use Internal Viewer" in the dialog).

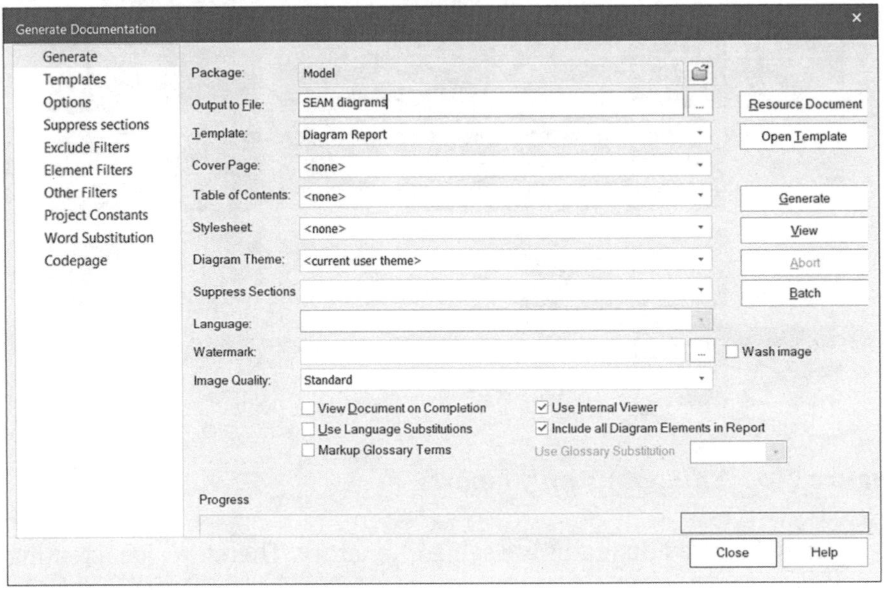

Figure 7-2. *Generating a diagrams-only document*

By default, Enterprise Architect gives every diagram a separate page
and adds some information such as the author, the created and modified
date, and the version number of the diagram (Figure 7-3). You can modify
this by changing the template in the "Generate Documentation" dialog.

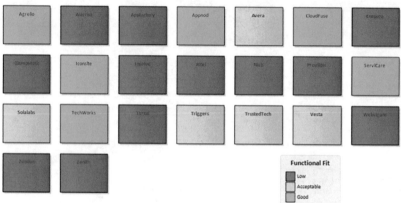

Figure 7-3. *A diagrams-only report*

Well-structured diagrams are self-explanatory. Therefore, just creating a report like this might already be sufficient to many stakeholders. But there is more information in the model that you might want to share, such as descriptions stored in the properties of the model elements.

RTF Reports

Note   The "Professional" version of Enterprise Architect does not allow you to work with the new "custom documents" and "dynamic content," so if you have this version, you have to rely on the old Report Builder.

Instead of creating a diagrams-only report, we can also choose to create a full RTF report (Figure 7-4). In the Ribbon, choose "Publish" ➤ "Report Builder" ➤ "Generate Documentation." Click "Generate," then "View."

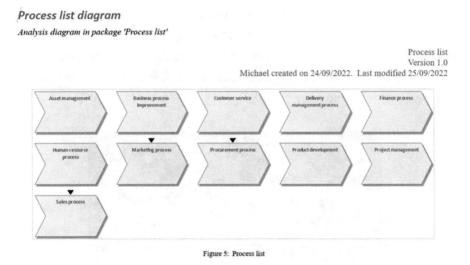

Figure 7-4. *RTF report containing the full model*

Of course, you can generate different documents for different audiences: a process list for the Systemplar Project Management Office (PMO), a business plan overview for executive management, or a list of IT systems for support. Just select the right package and template to generate the required document.

Also here, you can customize the look and feel of the document by changing the template. Open the template from the "Generate Documentation" dialog by clicking the "Open Template" button, then click the "Save as" button to save it under a different name.

Suppose Marketing provided us with a logo we should use in the footer of every document and a style guide prescribing the colors to use for titles and text (Figure 7-5). We will apply these, and also we change the contents of the template so that our tagged values for the applications will show up in the generated document.

Figure 7-5. *Systemplar's style guide*

Adding a Logo to the Footer

The Ribbon got an extra "Edit" tab when we opened the template. In this "Edit" tab, click "Edit" ➤ "Page Header and Footer." Drag the logo to the footer, change its alignment to right, and resize it so it does not take half a page (Figure 7-6). Once you are done, uncheck the "Edit Page Header and Footer."

Figure 7-6. *Adding the logo to the footer*

Changing the Color of the Main Title

Next, we will change the color of the titles in our document to bold orange (rgb 247, 106, 53), as per the style guide.

In the document template, select the {Pkg.Name} text. In the "Edit" tab of the Ribbon, select the Font color and click "More Colors" ➤ "Custom." Fill in the values 247, 106, and 53 for the Red, Green, and Blue colors, respectively. Click "OK" to confirm. The {Pkg.Name} will be bold orange from now on.

Even small changes like these can give a document a totally different feeling – in this case, more "Systemplar like."

Changing the Contents of the Report

Remember we spent some time adding information to the applications used by the Service department, contained in tagged values? The default template won't show these, because tagged values are excluded. Here is how to include them (Figure 7-7).

In the "Sections" part next to the template, unfold the "Package" and "Element." Check the box "Tagged Value," then right-click in the document on the {right-click-here-to-insert-Tagged-Value-field(s)}.

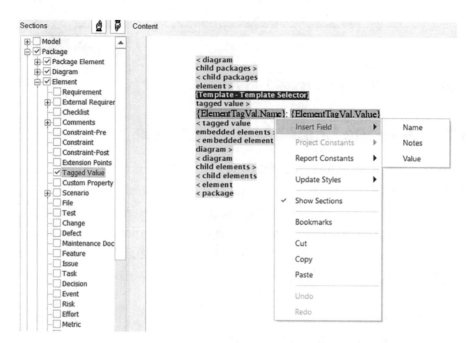

Figure 7-7. *Inserting tagged value fields in the report template*

Add both the tag name and the value and separate them with a colon (:).

Save the template and regenerate the document based on the new template, which is stored under "Custom Templates" in the Generate Documentation dialog (Figure 7-8).

Figure 7-8. *Document based on the new template*

164

CSV Exports

We already worked with csv exports in previous chapters, so let's quickly wrap up what we discussed there.

Basically, there are three ways to export data to a csv, each with their own advantages.

Exporting from List View

Open any diagram in the package with the Systemplar software list. In "Design," click "List View." The contents of the diagram are now shown as a list with default columns Name, Status, Type, and Modified.

You can add columns with the Field Chooser. Right-click the header of the list to view this Field Chooser.

Select any field from the Field Chooser and drag it to the header (Figure 7-9).

If you want to delete a column, drag it from the header to an empty space in the list (it shows a cross).

It is also possible to add tagged value columns. For example, suppose we would like to show our software list, indicating the functional fit score.

Select any element, right-click it, and click "Add Tag Value Column," then select the appropriate tagged value from the list – "FunctionalFit" in our case (Figure 7-10).

Figure 7-9. *Field Chooser*

Add Tag Value Column	×

Add a read only column to display the Tagged Value of an Element. Either type in the Tagged Value name or choose one from the list.

List Options

Specify how to fill the Tag Value list

○ Global Tagged Values

◉ Tagged Values from the selected Element

Tagged Value: FunctionalFit   ▾

Note: You can also add Tag Value columns by using drag drop from the Tag Values window.

OK	Cancel	Help

Figure 7-10. *Adding a tag value column*

Now simply select all elements in the list by keeping the Shift button pressed while pressing the arrow keys.

Press "Ctrl+C" to copy all selected elements, open a spreadsheet, and press "Ctrl+V."

The list will be exported to the spreadsheet application.

Since copying and pasting involves the clipboard, this also works with other target software.

Exporting with an Export Specification

A second way to export the contents of a package to CSV is by defining an export specification, which can be found in the Ribbon: "Publish" ➤ "CSV" ➤ "CSV Exchange Specification." After defining the specification, click "Publish" ➤ "CSV" ➤ "CSV Import/Export" and choose the specification.

Refer to Chapter 3 where we discussed this extensively.

Exporting a Relationship Matrix

As discussed in Chapter 4, you can export a matrix that shows relationships between elements. It is not possible to combine exporting element fields apart from Name and a Relationship Matrix, but you can export both separately and then use a function like *xlookup* in the spreadsheet to combine both exports. Just make sure the element names are unique.

A Website

The most powerful export option is no doubt the website export. This will not only allow you to publish every piece of information in the model, but it will preserve its structure and make all items clickable, so that you can easily navigate through the model. You only need to take care that the model is well structured.

Case 7-1: A Website for the Enterprise Architecture

We can safely put the SEAM in the open: after all, we only imported information that was readily available or not sensitive in any case. We just "connected the dots" by connecting elements to each other.

Therefore, we can export the model as a website and upload it on the public part of Systemplar's intranet.

Here's how to do that (Figure 7-11):

1. Make a version of the logo where the icon sits next to the company name and resize it so it would be 50 pixels high. Include this as the header image.

2. Indicate "Other Diagram" as the Default Diagram: the one with the navigation cells leading to the most important diagrams.

3. Choose a nice-looking theme "Ocean Breeze" with colors matching the Systemplar colors.

4. Then, click "Generate" and "View." (Figure 7-12)

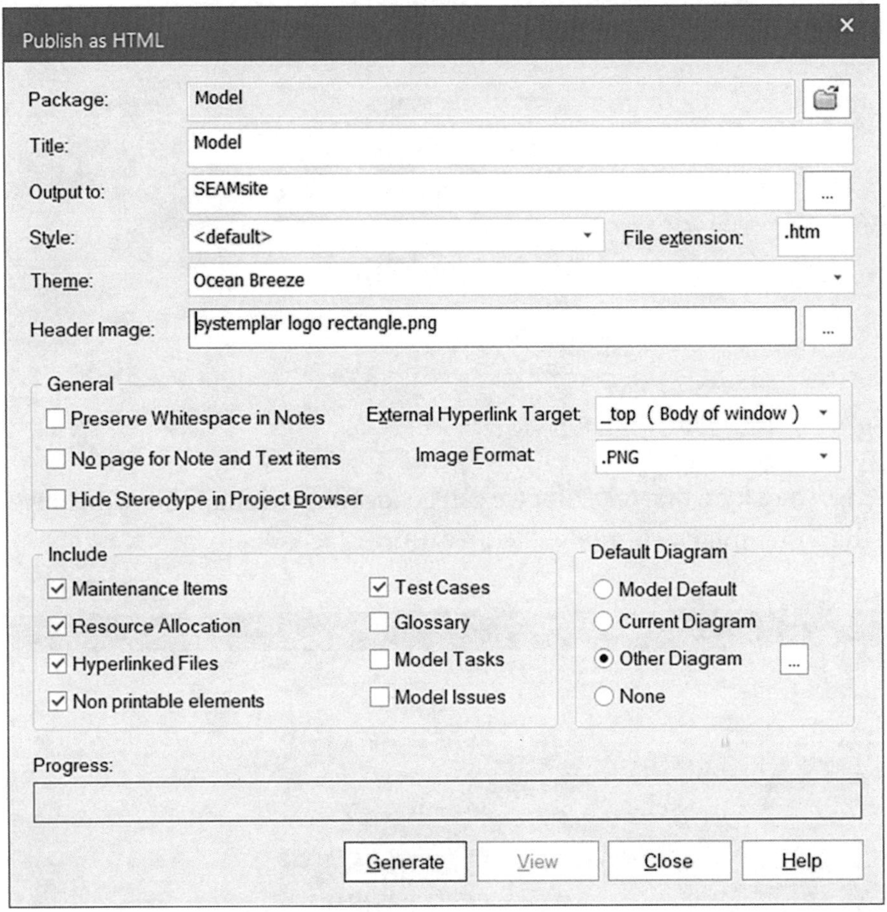

Publish as HTML   ×

Package:	Model	
Title:	Model	
Output to:	SEAMsite	...
Style:	<default> ▾	File extension: .htm
Theme:	Ocean Breeze	▾
Header Image:	systemplar logo rectangle.png	...

General

☐ Preserve Whitespace in Notes   External Hyperlink Target: _top (Body of window) ▾

☐ No page for Note and Text items   Image Format: .PNG ▾

☐ Hide Stereotype in Project Browser

Include   **Default Diagram**

☑ Maintenance Items   ☑ Test Cases   ○ Model Default

☑ Resource Allocation   ☐ Glossary   ○ Current Diagram

☑ Hyperlinked Files   ☐ Model Tasks   ◉ Other Diagram ...

☑ Non printable elements ☐ Model Issues   ○ None

Progress:

[Generate]   [View]   [Close]   [Help]

Figure 7-11. *Publish as HTML*

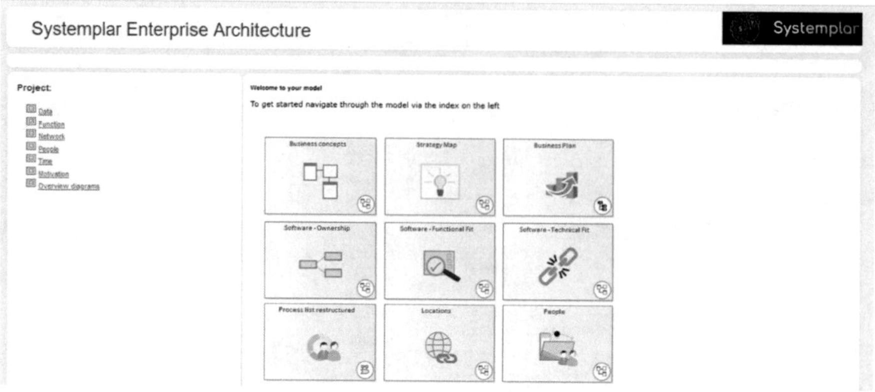

Figure 7-12. *The SEAM website*

Not bad for a first take! But we can go further and adapt the style fully to the Systemplar style guide (Figure 7-13).

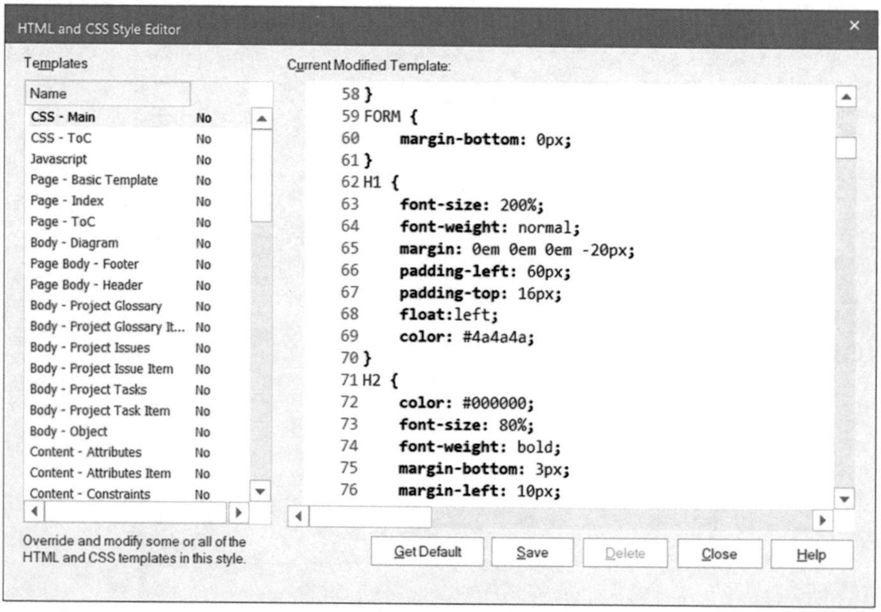

Figure 7-13. *Changing the HTML and CSS*

In the Resource browser, right-click the HTML Publishing item. Select "Create HTML Template." Make the necessary changes, for example, in the "CSS – Main," to reflect the colors of the style guide, then save it. The HTML template now shows up in the Resource Browser under "HTML Publishing." You can modify it from there by right-clicking it.

Then, in the "Publish as HTML" dialog, you can select the newly created template.

Note   In the same Resource Browser, you find other templates that are used by Enterprise Architect, such as the linked document templates, which can be changed as well.

Slideshows in the EA User Interface

If you regularly update diagrams in Enterprise Architect, you would have to update them in your presentations as well. Could you give a presentation directly from Enterprise Architect itself? Sure you can!

In the Ribbon, click "Start" ➤ "Design" ➤ "Focus" ➤ "Model Views." Right-click "Model Views" and select "New Slideshow." Give it an appropriate name (Figure 7-14).

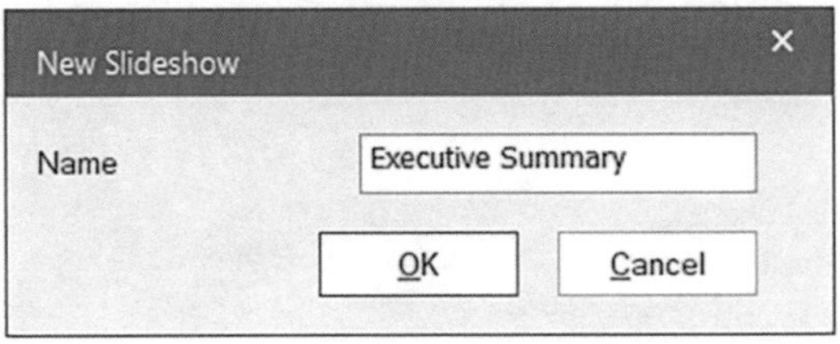

Figure 7-14. *New slideshow*

Double-click the slideshow to open its properties, such as name, whether autoplay should be enabled, and the time between slides if autoplay is on (Figure 7-15).

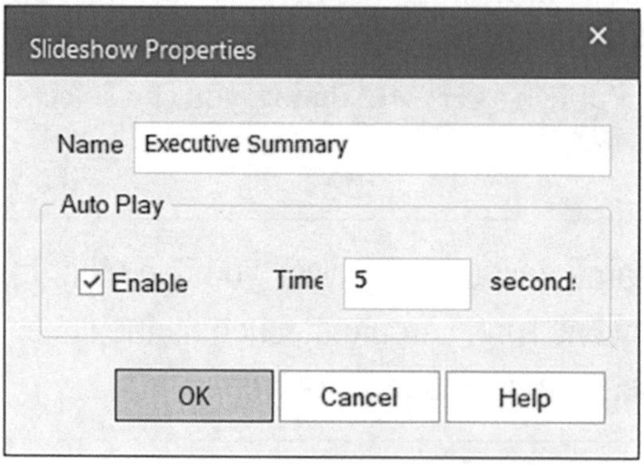

Figure 7-15. *Slideshow properties*

Next, you need to fill the slideshow with diagrams. Undock the Focus window from the Project Browser by selecting the "Focus" tab at the bottom and dragging it out of the menu. Then drag diagrams from the Project Browser to the slideshow folder you just created (Figure 7-16). For example, drag the Strategy Map, Strategy, and Business Plan diagrams to the Executive Summary folder so you can give an executive overview right away.

Browser

Project   Context   Diagram   Resources

◢ 🗊 Model
  ▷ 🗊 Data
  ▷ 🗊 Function
  ▷ 🗊 Network
  ▷ 🗊 People
  ▷ 🗊 Time
  ◢ 🗊 Motivation
    ◢ 🗀 Strategy
      🖽 Strategy
      🖽 Strategy Map

Focus

Working ...   Model Vi...   Quick Find   Revisit

◢ 🖻 Model Views
  ◢ 🞘 Executive Summary
    🖽 Strategy Map
    🖽 Strategy
    🖽 Business Plan
 ▷ 🖻 Recent
 ▷ 🗀 Library(s)

Figure 7-16. *A slideshow with slides*

As you can see, the Executive Summary slideshow contains links to the actual diagrams, so if their content changes, the slideshow does not need to be adapted.

To run the slideshow, right-click it in the Model Views and choose "Run Slideshow" or "Run Slideshow Fullscreen," the latter being probably what you want to do, since it hides the Enterprise Architect user interface so you can fully concentrate on the contents. If the settings are not on autoplay, you can get a control panel to steer the slideshow by clicking a diagram.

Summary

In this chapter, we discovered several ways to get information out of Enterprise Architect: by creating documents, websites, and even slideshows that can be started straight from the EA user interface. The next chapter will refine the SEAM by offering various ways to add custom information and to automate work by adding stereotypes.

CHAPTER 8

Tagged Values and Stereotypes

We as IT people can make progress, even if management doesn't understand it.

—John Zachman

Over the first seven chapters, we have covered all the basics of Enterprise Architect. The result is a fairly well-documented Enterprise Architecture model of a company. But we didn't spend any time on standardizing this work.

In the penultimate chapter of the book, we will do exactly that: discuss some features that keep the model consistent as it grows. We will take time to explore some more advanced features that rely on tagged values and stereotypes.

General Types

Elements in Enterprise Architect have out of the box already a fairly complete set of properties to store information, like Status, Difficulty, Priority, etc. Chances are that you will use these properties and that you discover you want them changed model-wide so that every contributor to

© Peter Doomen 2023
P. Doomen, *Introduction to SparxSystems Enterprise Architect*,
https://doi.org/10.1007/978-1-4842-9312-6_8

the project uses the same set of Statuses, Priorities, and the like. To access the General Types page, go to the Ribbon, click "Settings" ➤ "Model Types" ➤ "General Types" (Figure 8-1).

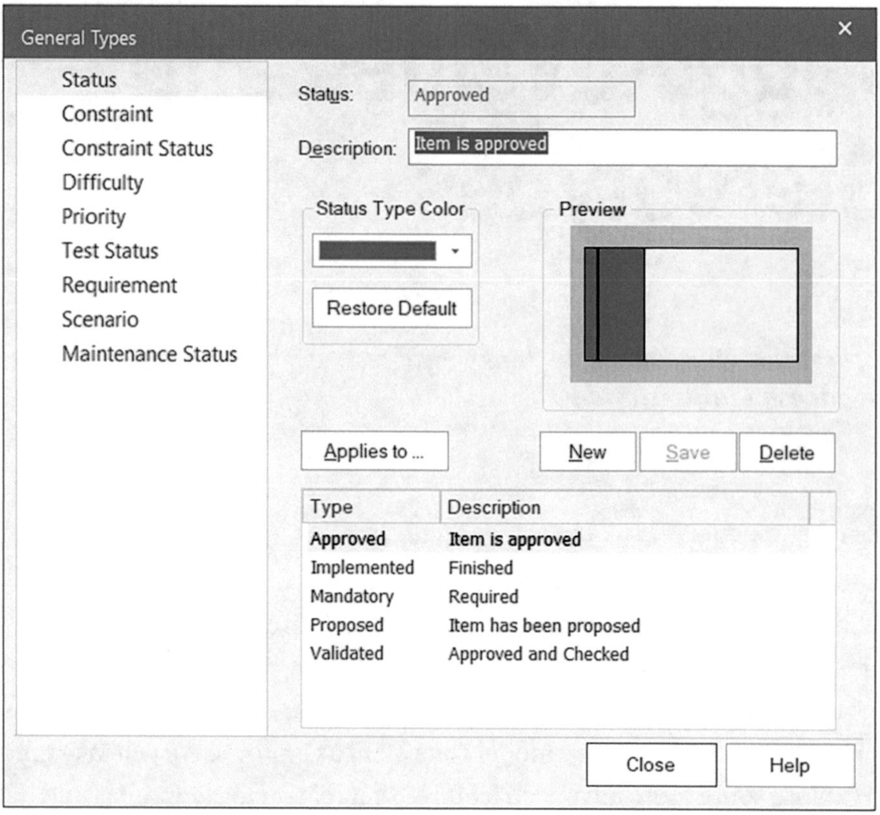

Figure 8-1. *General types*

Status

In this tab sheet, you can not only define your own set of statuses but also the status colors and the element types it applies to.

For me, the default list provided by Enterprise Architect makes sense:

- Proposed: The analyst has detected a potential requirement and adds it to the requirements package. This should be the default setting for a requirement.

- Approved: Business has looked into the requirement and verified it is required.

- Validated: The requirement is sufficiently validated to be implemented by the development team.

- Implemented: The software solution meets the requirement.

There is one exception: the status "mandatory" has nothing to do with status. A requirement can be mandatory ("required") and at the same time approved, validated, or implemented. I suggest removing "Mandatory" from this list.

If you need an additional status, you can click "New" to add it to the list.

Constraint and Constraint Status

Constraints put limits on things. In the context of Enterprise Architect, constraints are mainly used for documenting use cases and other functional and technical designs. So they are less relevant for our purposes. The same holds for constraint status, which is like the regular status but applies to constraints.

Some Enterprise Architect users complain that Constraints are too deeply hidden in the user interface. However, there is another way of showing Constraints in a more visual way.

This approach has the extra advantage that you can connect one constraint to more than one element. For example, suppose we would want to put a constraint that implements the business rule "First create the customer before you send invoices to that customer." This is a constraint on two business concepts ("customer" and "invoice" – Figure 8-2).

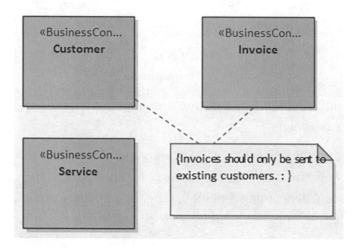

Figure 8-2. *Attaching visual constraints*

To visualize this constraint, right-click one of the concepts on a diagram, and choose "New Child Element" ➤ "Attach Constraint." Edit the constraint properties, and use the Quicklinker to attach it to the other element as well.

Difficulty

Difficulty gives a rough indication of how much work it costs to implement a certain item. It can be useful in the context of a business plan, where even if the different items of the business plan are still high level, they can be categorized according to how hard they are to implement.

The basic setting for difficulty has three levels: high, medium, and low. You can add or delete difficulty levels here and indicate which one should be the default.

Priority

Priority has by default three possible values: high, medium, and low.

Together with difficulty, the priority of items can be used to spot "low-hanging fruit": items with high priority and low difficulty.

Another useful overview is the combination of Status and Priority that shows whether the team is working on the right items. You can use the Inspector Window to see the requirements together with their status and priority (Figure 8-3):

1. Activate the diagram with the business plan containing the Origa requirements by clicking it in the Project Browser.

2. Activate the Inspector Window: in the Ribbon, click "Start" ➤ "Design" ➤ "Inspect."

3. Show the Status tab by clicking "Status."

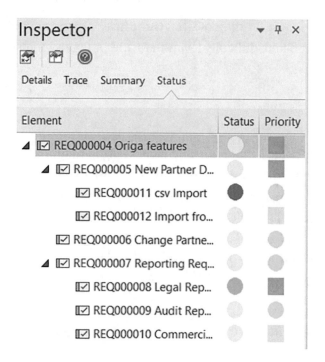

Figure 8-3. *Inspector Status view*

The colors of the priority levels and the indicator icon (square, circle, etc.) can be changed in the General Types window.

Test Status

If you use Enterprise Architect for managing tests, you can change the values of the Test Status here. This is also less relevant for documenting an enterprise architecture.

Requirement

Using Enterprise Architect for business analysis could be a logical continuation from the business plan. A classical way to describe what a product must be able to do is by writing requirements.

There are two types of requirements: functional (what the product must be able to do) and nonfunctional (qualities the product must have). A very well-developed framework for business analysis is the Volere method by James and Suzanne Robertson (`www.volere.org`).

If you want to use Enterprise Architect for this purpose, I suggest you replace the default requirements list by this list (headings only, the description is given so you know what falls under each of the high-level requirements):

- Functional: They describe the functions the product has to perform to support the business process.

- Look and feel: Appearance and style requirements.

- Usability and humanity: Ease of use, personalization, internationalization, learning, understandability, politeness, accessibility, convenience.

- Performance: Speed and latency, safety critical, precision and accuracy, reliability and availability, robustness and fault tolerance, capacity, scalability and extensibility, longevity.

- Operational and environmental: Expected physical environment, wider environment, interfacing with adjacent systems, productization, release, backward compatibility.

- Maintainability and support: Maintenance, supportability, adaptability.

- Security: Access, integrity, privacy, audit, immunity.

- Cultural: Cultural market, cultural diversity and inclusion.

- Compliance: Legal compliance, standards compliance.

Scenario

Useful if you use Enterprise Architect for functional modeling, such as use cases. The scenarios provide a way to structure these.

Maintenance Status

If you use Enterprise Architect for technical work, such as keeping an overview of maintenance tasks on applications, you can adapt this list of statuses to your needs. Less applicable for documenting an enterprise architecture.

Tagged Values

If the default properties of elements are not enough for your needs, then you can further adapt Enterprise Architect by using tagged values. In essence, a tagged value is a field that can be attached to any element or connector. It consists of a tag name and a value.

For example, in Chapter 4 we extended the software list with the notions of "FunctionalFit," "TechnicalFit," and "Ownership," all three of which are not present in the standard properties list. "FunctionalFit" is the tag, "4" a possible value. Adding tags allows you thus to keep extra information about elements and connectors in a very intuitive way.

Adding a Tagged Value

Like we discussed in Chapter 4, any element (and connector) can have a number of tagged values attached to it. As a quick reminder, adding a tagged value is easy: open the properties window, choose the tab "Tags," and click the "New" button. Then fill in the tag name and value.

Exporting Tagged Values

We also discussed how to export the tagged values along with the other element properties. Remember there are two ways of achieving this:

- Open the diagram in List View (Ribbon: "Design"), then right-click the header and choose the tagged values to be included. When it shows the appropriate columns, just select the rows to be exported and press "Ctrl+C." In the target application, such as a spreadsheet, press "Ctrl+V" to paste.

- Make a csv export specification, include tagged value columns there, and use the csv export from the Ribbon "Publish" tab.

Applying to Multiple Items

If you need to attach a tagged value to multiple items, it would be cumbersome to open them one by one, each time adding the tag and the value separately. There is a much faster way of doing this: select the items you want to attach the tag to, and press "Ctrl+Shift+T." This opens the dialog window "Tagged Value." Now just type the tag name and the value, and confirm with "OK" (Figure 8-4).

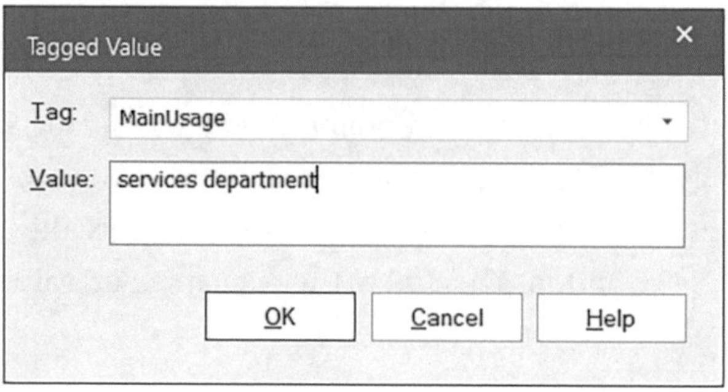

Figure 8-4. *Tagged value dialog*

Case 8-1: Adding Custom Information to the Enterprise Architecture Model

Chances are that you want to involve other architects when building complicated models such as the SEAM. There are two actions you can take if you want people to work together such that all deliver likewise results:

- Developing a toolbox that guides the Systemplar employees in refining the SEAM. This makes sure all of them use the same elements and connectors. This will be discussed in the next chapter.

- Including Tagged Field Types to some of the elements, so that it would become clear what information is required for which elements. This will be the subject of the current chapter.

As a first step, we will define some global tagged values. Then we define Tagged Value Types for these, where we can limit the values they can take. For example, we will provide a field that indicates if an application is customer facing or not. The allowable values would be "true" and "false."

Local vs. Global Tagged Values

While you can work with tagged values that are created locally, it is often better to define them globally so that they are available to anyone in the whole of the model.

Here is how to do this. Suppose we want to add lifecycle management to our software list. An application can be in any of these states:

- Acquire/Develop: Buying or developing the software to first usage.

- Mature: From the moment the application is considered fit for production.

- Retiring: Plans are being made to replace the application.

- Retired: The application is no longer supported.

We can define a tagged value "LifecycleStage" (Figure 8-5):

1. In the Ribbon, choose "Settings" ➤ "UML Types."

2. Click "Tagged Value Types," then add the tag name and description.

3. Click "Save."

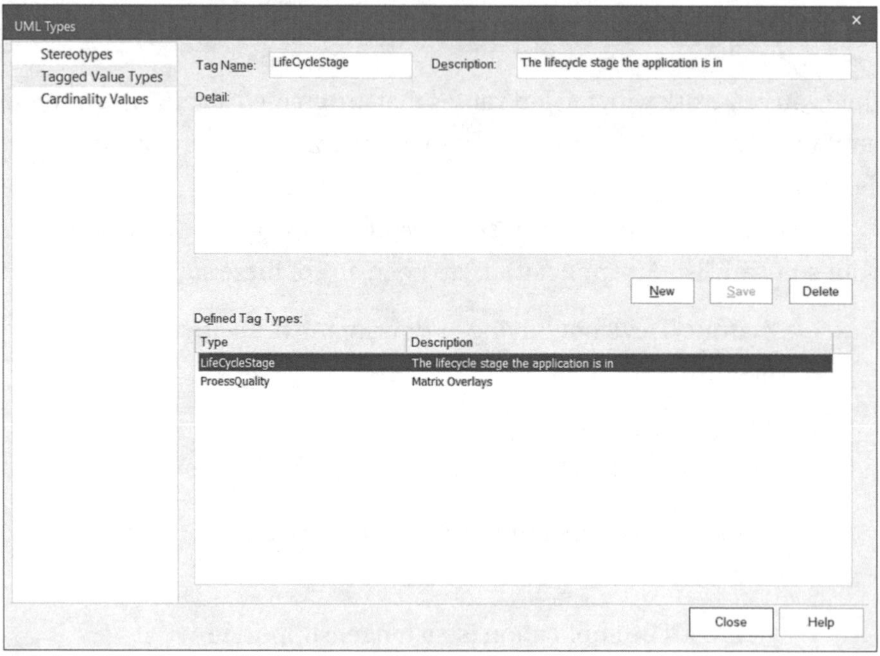

Figure 8-5. *Defining a tagged value type*

As a next step, we would like to limit the possible states to the four we mentioned earlier.

4. Click the LifeCycleStage in the list of Defined Tag Types. Then add these lines to the "Details" field (Figure 8-6):

```
Type=Drop down;
```

```
Values=Acquire/Develop, Mature, Retiring,
Retired;
```

5. Click "Save." Time to test it!

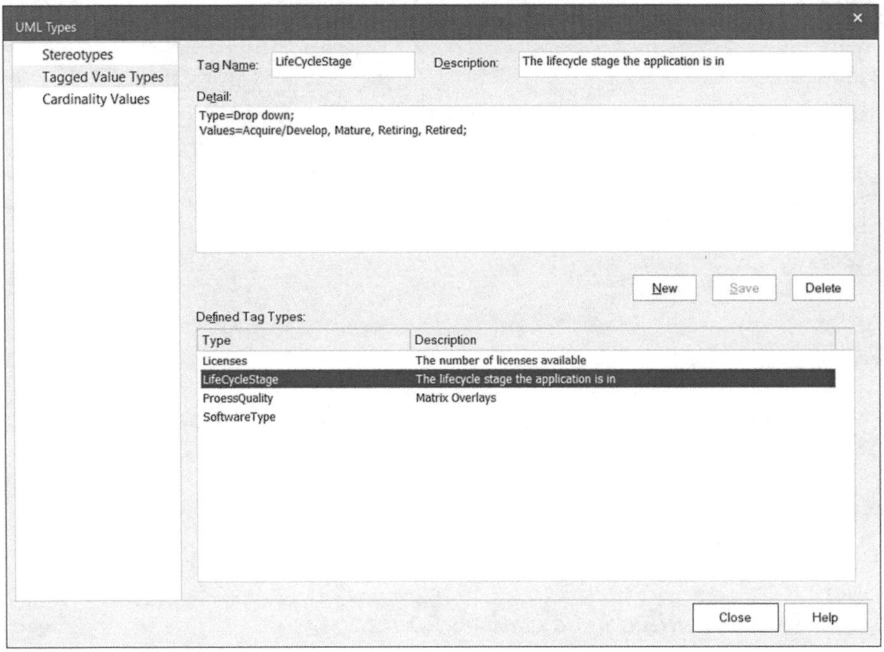

Figure 8-6. *Lifecycle stages as values for a drop-down box*

6. Open the properties of an application.

7. Add the tagged value "LifeCycleStage" from the list (type "life" to limit the drop down to only tagged values containing that string).

8. Close the dialog box.

9. Now the value field of the LifeCycleStage shows a down arrow, indicating you can pick its value from a list.

10. Just pick a value and confirm with "OK" (Figure 8-7).

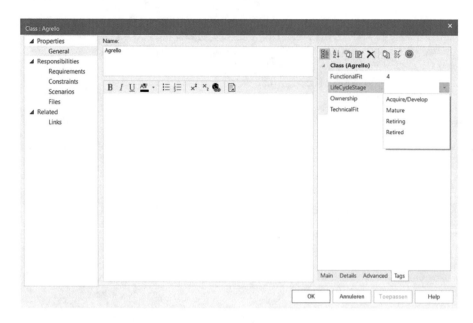

Figure 8-7. *A limited list as values for a tag*

Dealing with Numeric Values

Suppose you have a numeric value, such as the number of licenses
Systemplar bought for each application (Figure 8-8). You can then create
a tagged value type "Licenses" and limit the possible values from 0 to 1000
by adding this in the detail field:

```
Type=Spin;

UpperBound=1000;

LowerBound=0;

Default=0;
```

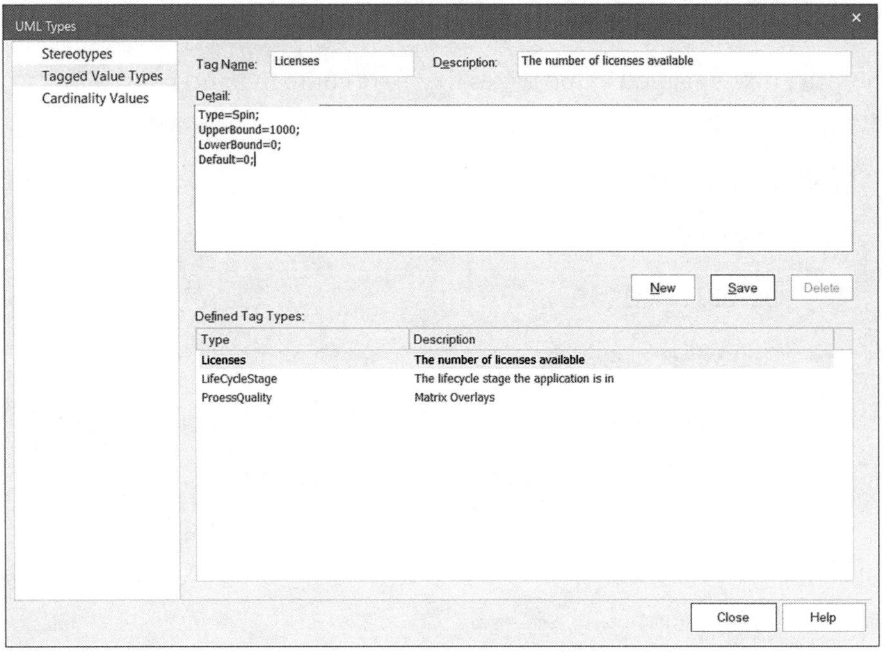

Figure 8-8. *A numeric value between 0 and 1000 as values for a tag*

Numeric values can also be defined as

- Type=Float;

- Type=Decimal;

- Type=Double;

- Type=Integer;

where a default value is specified with Default=Val;.

Additional Tagged Value Types

There are other Tagged Value Types that may come in handy. Just a few, with an example:

- CustomerFacing

  ```
  Type=Boolean;
  ```

  ```
  Default=False;
  ```

- SoftwareType

  ```
  Type=CheckList;
  ```

  ```
  Values=AdministrativeService, Operational,
  Critical;
  ```

or

  ```
  Type=Enum;
  ```

  ```
  Values=AdministrativeService, Operational,
  Critical;
  ```

  ```
  Default=AdministrativeService;
  ```

- DateFirstUse

  ```
  Type=Date;
  ```

- StartTime

  ```
  Type=Time;
  ```

- ShortDescription

  ```
  Type=String;
  ```

  ```
  Default=Val;
  ```

- LongDescription

  ```
  Type=Memo;
  ```

- ProductPage

  Type=URL;

  Default=Val;

Note   While you can use the shortcut "Ctrl+Shift+T" to add the tag name of restricted tagged values, you cannot use it to add the value. If a tagged value has a default, it will be filled in as a value for all elements. If there is no default, it will be empty and you will have to specify a value for each element separately.

Stereotypes

A last mechanism used to tailor Enterprise Architect to your needs we will discuss in this chapter is that of stereotypes. A stereotype is a property of an element or a connector that can totally change the way the element or connector appears on a diagram.

So far, we have mainly used "classes" for documenting the SEAM. We used them for software, business concepts, locations, and even people! There is nothing wrong with that, but if you put more than one type of element on a diagram, it is hard to discern these elements.

Suppose we want to document which business concepts are realized with which applications. We could easily draw a diagram like Figure 8-9.

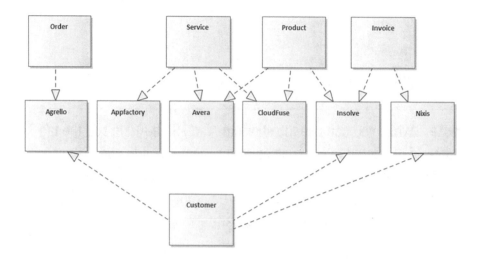

Figure 8-9. *Relations between business concepts and software*

While this diagram might be correct and nearly clutterless, it is still hard to read. Wouldn't it be more readable when the software classes were drawn somewhat differently than the business concepts? Even a slight change in color would make this diagram easier to understand.

We could do this on a diagram level by just selecting the software classes and giving them some other color. But if we want to achieve some consistency (say, software always drawn in blue colors, business concepts in green), we could define this on the model level.

The trick is to assign stereotypes, then tell Enterprise Architect how to render elements with these stereotypes.

As a first step, define the stereotypes <<BusinessConcept>> and <<Application>> (Figure 8-10).

Then, assign the stereotype <<BusinessConcept>> to the business concepts and <<application>> to the applications. The easiest way to do this is in list view: in the Ribbon, go to "Design" ➤ "List View," then right-click the header and open the Field Chooser. Drag the "Stereotype" column to the header. Click the three dots next to the stereotype of the first business concept, and choose "All Perspectives" ➤ Profile: "<none>". Then check the BusinessConcept stereotype. Do this for all business concepts and applications.

Note   The double brackets << >> indicate that the name between them is a stereotype.

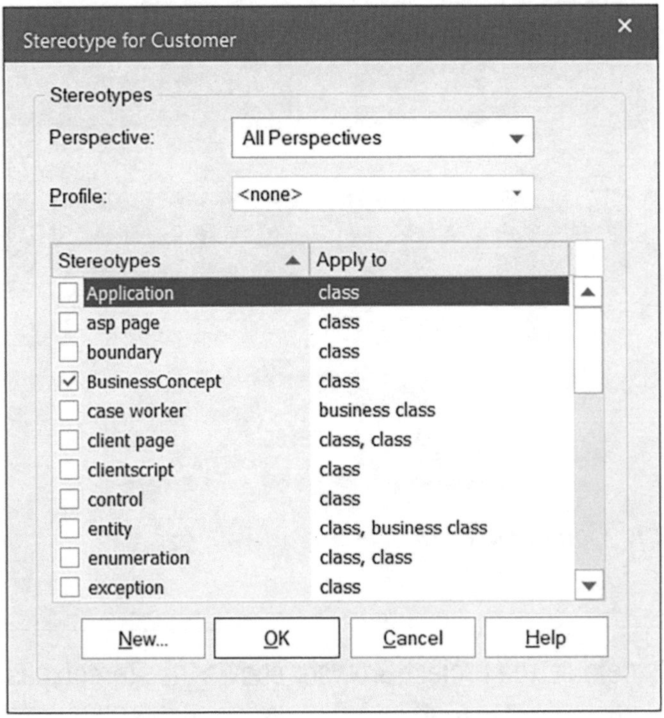

Figure 8-10. *Adding stereotypes to elements*

As a next step, we would like to give each stereotype its own appearance.

We turn to the UML Types dialog again. In the Ribbon, click "Settings" ➤ "UML Types." In the "Stereotypes" tab, select the <<application>> stereotype. As default colors, select pale blue for "Fill" and dark blue for "Border" and "Font." Click "Save."

Do the same for the <<businessconcept>> stereotype, but choose green colors for this one.

Click "Save" and verify the colors on the diagram have changed. Even a relatively simple color change can make diagrams like these easier to understand, as you can see in Figure 8-11.

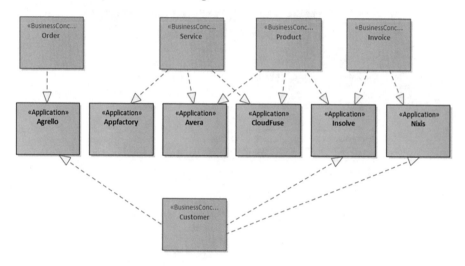

Figure 8-11. *Colors based on stereotype*

Note   By default, the Project Browser shows the stereotypes before the element's name. You can turn this off. Go to the Ribbon "Start" ➤ "Preferences" ➤ "General" ➤ "Show stereotypes." You need to restart Enterprise Architect to make this effective.

While our improved diagram is already nice, we still can go much further. There are two extension mechanisms that allow us to give elements and connectors any appearance we can imagine. The first is based on external metatypes and the second on the internal scripting language of Enterprise Architect, called Shape Script.

Overriding Appearance with Metatypes

If you need to show elements as a specific graphical element without text, you can attach a "Metafile" to the stereotype definition.

Suppose we want a representation of the Systemplar company in our model. We define the <<systemplar>> stereotype and attach the company logo as an emf file to the stereotype definition (Figure 8-12).

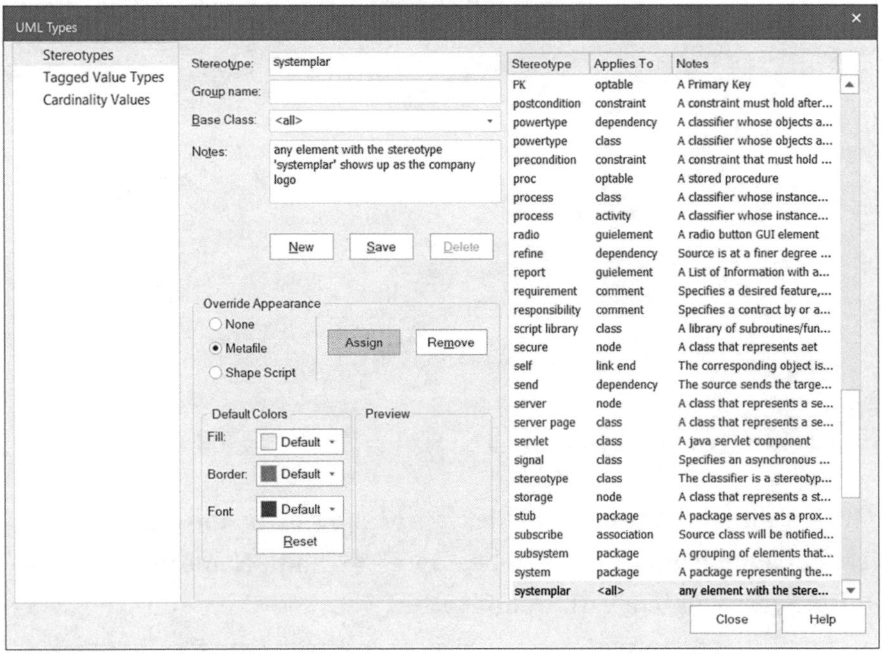

Figure 8-12. *Attaching a metafile to a stereotype*

Now if we include any element with the <<systemplar>> stereotype in a diagram, the result looks like Figure 8-13.

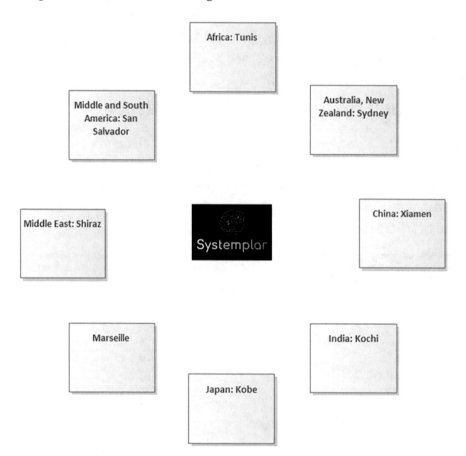

Figure 8-13. *Using a metafile*

If you still want the name of the class to show up on the diagram, right-click the element and choose "Appearance" ➤ "Show Name under Image."

Tip: Search for "convert to emf" to find websites where you can convert any graphic to emf format. You could also work with wmf files, but emf is an enhanced version so it is better to use this instead.

Overriding Appearance with Shape Script

While a full-blown discussion of Shape Script would require an entire book, a short introduction to the Shape Script language will suffice for our purposes.

Note

- Thomas Kilian has written such a book. You can find it at `https://leanpub.com/shapescript`.

- Another excellent resource is Geert Bellekens GitHub Repository with the definitions of all Shape Scripts that come standard with Enterprise Architect, which you can find here: `https://github.com/GeertBellekens/Enterprise-Architect-Shapescript-Library/`.

- Shapescripting is one of the most difficult features of Enterprise Architect, worsened by the fact that it is quite buggy. Several features simply don't work (I will give an example later) or don't work as expected. You have been warned.

A Simple Shape Script for Locations

Suppose we want to show the locations as ovals with the name of the location printed in the middle.

First, we define a stereotype "location" in the Ribbon: "Settings" ➤ "UML Types" ➤ "General Types" ➤ "Stereotypes." Then we add the stereotype to each of the locations.

If you need to apply a stereotype to lots of elements, you can create a csv export definition, export the elements, do the mass update in a spreadsheet application, and reimport them. For our small list of locations, however, doing it by hand in list view is easier and faster.

Now we add a Shape Script definition to the stereotype definition. In the UML Types dialog, click the location stereotype. In the section "Override Appearance," choose "Shape Script" and click "Edit." You get the Shape Editor window.

The actual "drawing" of stereotypes happens on a virtual canvas that comprises 100 units in both directions. The top-left coordinate is (0|0) and the bottom right (100|100).

Note   In reality, this is only a quarter of the full canvas. The other three quarters allow you to define "overlapping" shapes: shapes that partially overlap with other shapes. This is mainly used for defining connectors. You can spot these when you encounter negative coordinates.

Figure 8-14. *Defining a Shape Script*

This Shape Script will do the trick (Figure 8-14). Let's find out what it is composed of.

Shape Main

This tells Enterprise Architect that you are defining the "main" shape for a Shape Script (you can also add subshapes, compartments, and decorations):

```
shape main
{
...
}
```

The syntax of Shape Script is C++ like. The curly brackets encapsulate the rest of the "code."

Initializations

These commands must come up front, before you start "drawing":

```
noshadow=true;
v_align="center";
h_align="center";
fixedaspectratio=true;
defsize(80,80);
```

They define

- noshadow: If the shape gets a shadow, that gives it a 3D-like appearance on a diagram.

- v_align and h_align: How the text, if any, should be aligned vertically and horizontally.

- Fixedaspectratio: If the height and width should keep their relative size. Does not work, or, as Thomas Kilian puts it, YAEAB ("yet another EA bug").

- Defsize: The default size when you create a new element with this stereotype.

The Drawing Commands

These commands start, draw, and finish the drawing:

```
startpath();
ellipse(0,0,100,100);
endpath();
strokepath();
```

The Text Command

```
printwrapped("#NAME#");
```

This prints the element's name wrapped in the center of the ellipse. Enterprise Architect doesn't care if you write "printwrapped" or "print": in both cases, the text gets wrapped in the main shape. Of course, you can equally use other fields like alias, author, complexity, datecreated, datemodified, keywords, language, metatype, name, notes, scope, status, stereotype, and type.

The result of applying the Shape Script to the location stereotype is this. As you can see, the fixedaspectratio command fails (Figure 8-15).

Figure 8-15. *Shape Script applied to locations*

Some More Connector Linked Shape Script Commands

There is a whole list of Shape Script drawing commands you can use. Here are the main ones:

- MoveTo(x,y): Moves the cursor to the coordinates given by x and y.

- LineTo(x,y): Draws a line from the current location to the x and y specified and sets the new location to these values. Together with MoveTo, you can draw complex polygons.

- BezierTo(xStart, yStart, xBend, yBend, xEnd, yEnd): Draws a bezier line that will be bent toward xBend and yBend.

- Arc(left,top,right,bottom,xStart,yStart,xEnd,yEnd): Draws an arc with the parameters provided. If the command is ArcTo, it will also set the cursor position, otherwise not.

- RoundRect(left,top,right,bottom,cornerWidth,corn erHeight): A rounded rectangle where the size of the corners is given in absolute pixels, so they won't scale.

- Polygon(xCenter,yCenter,numberOfSides,radius,ro tation): A polygon with rotation as a floating value, counter-clockwise.

- StartCloudPath(puffWidth,puffHeight,noise): Identical to StartPath but this one draws puffy lines. The puffiness can be steered with the parameters.

- FillAndStrokePath(): Used instead of StrokePath(). Will not only draw a border but also fill the inside.

- DrawNativeShape(): Instead of drawing something, it draws the form the element would get without Shape Script. This is frequently used in combination with if HasTag(tagName) or HasTag(tagName,tagValue) to draw a special form if some tag/value is present, having the normal shape as a default. Idem for HasProperty(<property>) and HasProperty(<property>,<value>).

An Example of a Shape Script Applied to Connectors

Although the working and the effect of connector stereotype Shape Script is largely the same as the element's counterpart, there are a few differences:

- Connector stereotypes consist mostly of three parts: the source element part, the connector line itself, and the target element part.

- Connectors have six default labels that you can use to show information. These are the source bottom label, source top label, middle bottom label, middle top label, target bottom label, and target top label. The general command to print information to these is print("LeftTopLabel") and to hide them HideLabel(LeftTopLabel). You don't need to use ShowLabel(LeftTopLabel) because the label automatically shows when you assign content to it.

- Some commands make no sense when defining connector stereotype Shape Scripts, such as drawing other things than lines as connectors. That is not to say this is impossible, but the results are weird and I don't see a use for it.

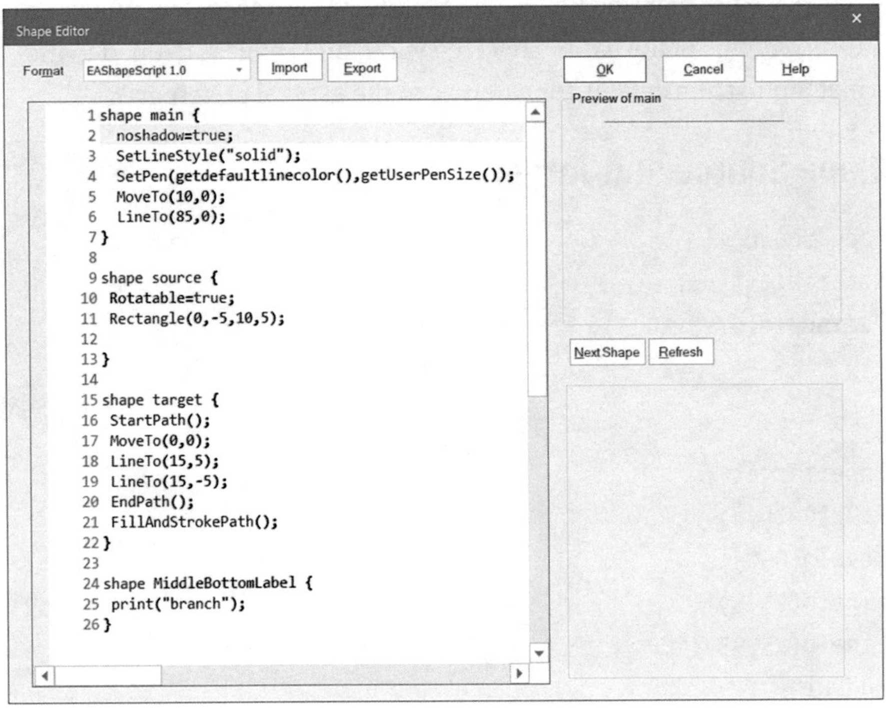

Figure 8-16. *Adding stereotypes to connectors*

When defining connector stereotype Shape Scripts, you can "move" through the different parts in the preview by clicking "Next Shape" under the preview window (Figure 8-16).

Shape Main

```
shape main {
  noshadow=true;
  SetLineStyle("solid");
  SetPen(getdefaultlinecolor(),getUserPenSize());
  MoveTo(10,0);
  LineTo(85,0);
}
```

Here, we basically tell Enterprise Architect to render as a connector a simple solid line of the user's preferred width and color, as defined in the format toolbar, the default appearance, or the general preferences.

Shape Source and Target

```
shape source {
  Rotatable=true;
  Rectangle(0,-5,10,5);

}

shape target {
  StartPath();
  MoveTo(0,0);
  LineTo(15,5);
  LineTo(15,-5);
  EndPath();
  FillAndStrokePath();
}
```

The shape at the source of the connector will be a rectangle; at the target, we get an arrow.

Label Shapes

To avoid the label showing an ugly <<isbranch>> on the diagram, we replace it by the simple word "branch." (Figure 8-17) Or we could hide it by stating HideLabel(MiddleBottomLabel):

```
shape MiddleBottomLabel {
  print("branch");
}
```

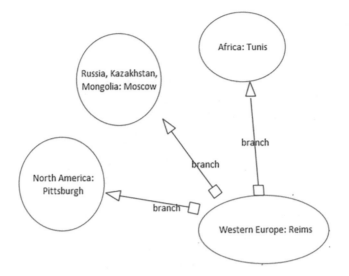

Figure 8-17.   *Connector Shape Scripts in action*

Stereotypes and Shape Scripts will become much more useful if you combine them with developing your own toolbox, which is the subject of the last chapter. Hold on!

Summary

In this chapter, we covered some more advanced features of Enterprise Architect, such as different methods to add custom information to the model or to change the rendering of elements and connectors on diagrams by adding scripting or metafiles. The next chapter will deal with even more advanced stuff, eventually leading to a custom toolbox.

CHAPTER 9

Your Own Toolbox

EA is not a quick fix, it's another way of living.

—John Zachman

This final chapter will teach you how to create a custom toolbox that implements the metamodel we used so far for the SEAM. This is useful to gain time but also to put standards in place, especially if there are multiple people working on the same model. There is a lot to say about this topic, and we will just scratch the surface of it, but it will be an eye opener even for experienced EA users. We will start with a very simple toolbox, gradually adding more features such as adding Shape Scripts, tagged values, and diagram properties.

Case 9-1: Leaving the Enterprise Architecture Model for the Architects of the Company

To create and test a toolbox, we will create a separate root node called "Toolbox," with two folders (Figure 9-1):

- A folder with the actual toolbox ("Toolbox v1," to keep versions of the toolbox separate)

- A test folder ("Test") where we can safely experiment with this newly created toolbox

© Peter Doomen 2023
P. Doomen, *Introduction to SparxSystems Enterprise Architect*,
https://doi.org/10.1007/978-1-4842-9312-6_9

The "toolbox" view under the root node "toolbox" will get the stereotype "Profile" and a diagram of type "Class."

This tells Enterprise Architect to open the "Profile" toolbox that contains all elements necessary to create a toolbox.

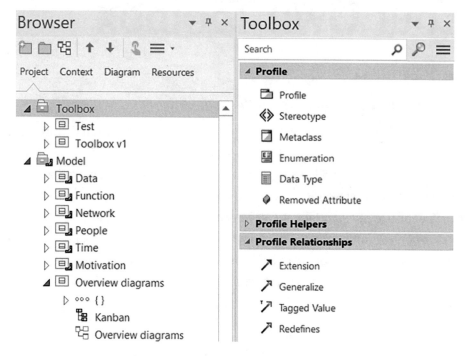

Figure 9-1. *A root node for our toolbox*

Next, we will define the metaclass from which we will derive the elements in our toolbox. This is simply done by adding a metaclass called "Class" to the toolbox diagram.

Then, we define the elements themselves:

1. For each element, add a "stereotype" element to the diagram and name it appropriately (name of the element).

2. For each stereotype, draw an "extension" relationship to the metaclass.

3.   Optionally, change the default color of each
     stereotype to the default color of the elements
     (green for BusinessConcepts, blue for Software).

4.   The result can be seen in Figure 9-2.

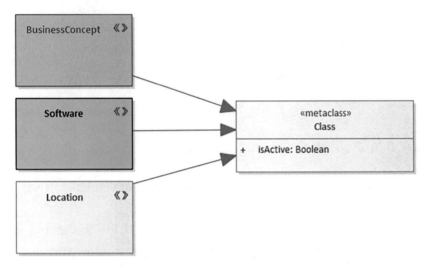

Figure 9-2.   *Simple toolbox definition*

This is already enough to create a toolbox, import it, and test it.

Exporting and Importing the Toolbox

Publishing the package so that it can be imported as a toolbox can be
achieved via the Ribbon: "Specialize" ➤ "Publish Technology" ➤ "Publish
Package as a UML Profile." (Attention: It is indeed the "Specialize" tab
you need to activate, not the "Publish" one). There you simply specify a
name and location and click "Save" to export the toolbox specification
(Figure 9-3).

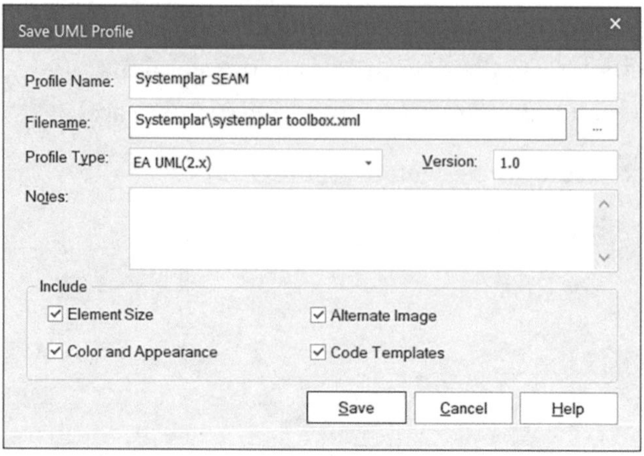

Figure 9-3. *Publish the package as a UML profile*

The next step is to import it again. This is done totally differently from the export.

Go to the "Resources" window, look for the "UML Profiles" entry, and right-click it. Select "Import UML Profile…." A dialog window appears, where you can look up the toolbox specification and click "Import" to import it.

As you can verify from the "Resources" window, the Systemplar SEAM toolbox has been imported. We can test it from here: just go to the Project Browser and create a class diagram under the test folder. Then activate the diagram, go to the "Resources" window again, and drag any of the toolbox elements to the diagram.

The toolbox works, as you can see in Figure 9-4: you can add elements to a diagram, and they get a default name and appearance. Let's further refine this toolbox so that it does exactly what it needs to do.

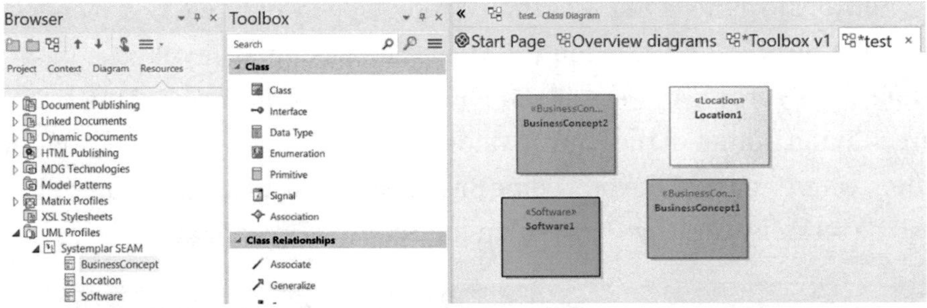

Figure 9-4. *Testing the toolbox*

Adding a Shape Script

As a first step, we will add the Shape Script to the "location" element. To achieve this goal, we need to add an attribute to the "location" stereotype named "_image" (with underscore) and give this an initial value equal to the Shape Script:

```
shape main{
 noshadow=true;
 v_align="center";
 h_align="center";
 fixedaspectratio=true;
 defsize(80,80);
 startpath();
 ellipse(0,0,100,100);
 endpath();
 strokepath();
 printwrapped("#NAME#");
}
```

Add an attribute to the "Location" stereotype by right-clicking it and choosing "Features" ➤ "Attributes." The attribute should be called "_image" (Figure 9-5). Leave all other fields as they are, and click the three-dotted button in the "Initial Value" field. This opens the Shape Script editor, where you add the preceding Shape Script. As you know, you can test the script by clicking "Refresh" in the Shape Script editor.

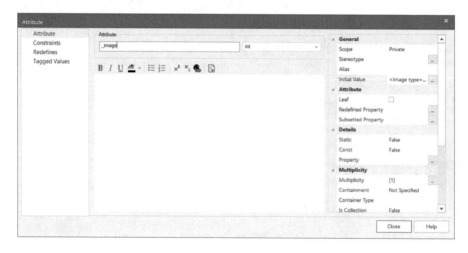

Figure 9-5. *Location Shape Script defining the image*

Now just export and import the toolbox, overwriting the existing one. Then reopen the test diagram, which is automatically updated with the new Shape Script (Figure 9-6).

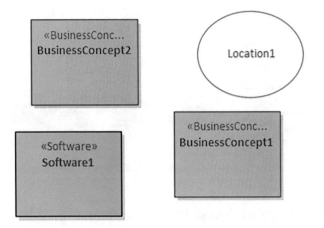

Figure 9-6. *Toolbox with a Shape Script*

Note   This is actually one of the big benefits of working with custom stereotypes and Shape Sscripts – if you ever change minds about how the elements should look like, it is easy to update them all at once.

Default Size

You can easily specify a default size for newly created elements by adding these attributes and giving them an initial value that indicates the default:

- _sizeX: The width of the element

- _sizeY: The height of the element

If you don't add these size attributes, the default of 100 applies.

In this example, we specified a _sizeY attribute for the software element with "50" as an initial value. If you now export the toolbox and import it, you will see that the existing diagram element "Software1" has not changed. To test it, add a new element of type "Software" (Figure 9-7).

215

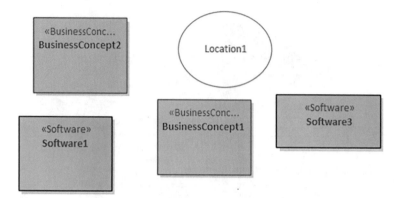

Figure 9-7. *Specifying default width and height*

This is of course the desired behavior: the default gets applied at element creation time. Changes afterward should be possible!

The Profile Helper

Up till now, we have been creating our toolbox the old, manual way. But there is a nifty tool in Enterprise Architect to help us: the Profile Helper (Figure 9-8). It is actually a kind of wizard or better a set of wizards that you can reach via the toolbox:

- MDG Technology: An MDG technology (short for Model-Driven Generation technology) is a bundle of stereotypes, toolboxes, patterns, diagrams, and other related entities that work together to create customized extensions of UML.

- Add Stereotype: The one you will use most – it allows you to create individual toolbox elements, basically what we did in the preceding paragraphs.

- Create Custom Toolbox: Mainly used if you want to add submenus to the toolbox.

- Add Toolbox Page: Create an actual toolbox page so you can drag elements from the toolbox to a diagram.

- Add Diagram Extension: Used to include new diagram types based on existing ones.

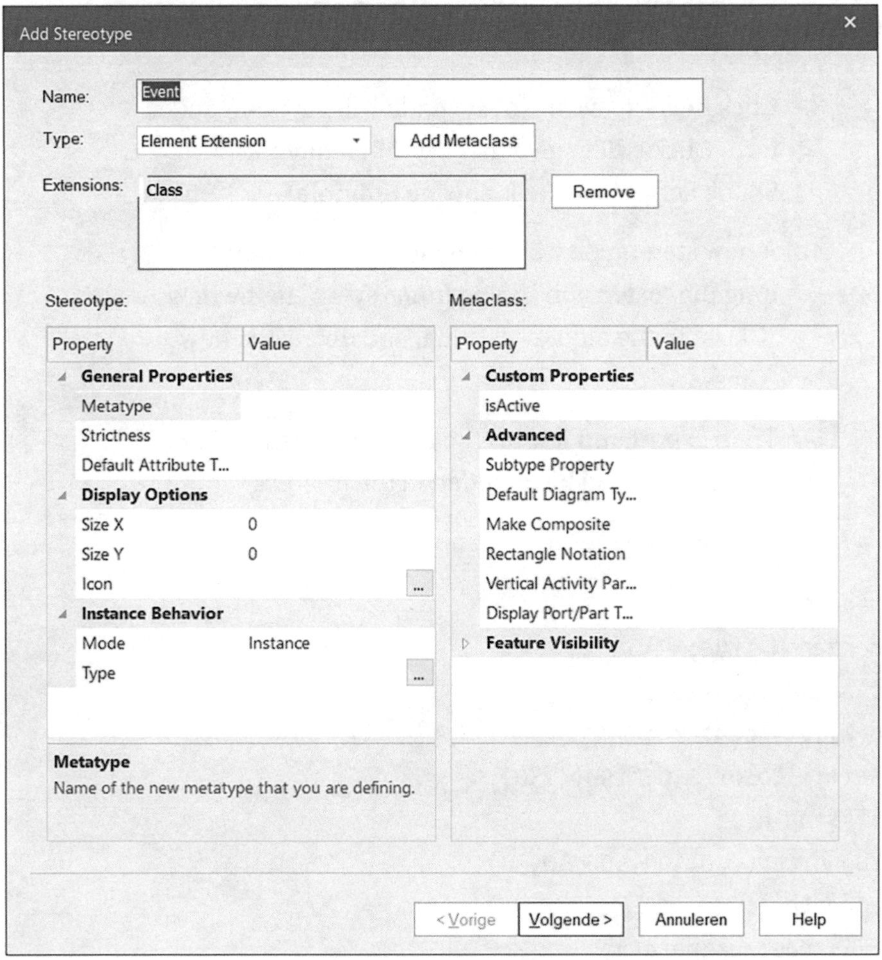

Figure 9-8. *Adding a stereotype with the stereotype helper*

We will use the "Add Stereotype" helper to create a new element type "event." This is rather straightforward:

1. Drag the "Add Stereotype" helper from the toolbox to the toolbox definition diagram. A wizard appears.

2. Fill in the name ("event") and the metaclass ("class").

3. Click next – leave the next window like it is, and click next. Click edit to give the "event" element its own Shape Script (see the following example).

4. A new stereotype will be created. You can now drag the "extension" going from "event" to the new "Class" to the already existing, and delete the new "Class."

5. Then export and import the toolbox as usual. The "event" type will be included in the toolbox.

A first version of the "event" Shape Script:

```
shape main{
 noshadow=true;
 v_align="center";
 h_align="center";
 setfillcolor(150, 150, 150);
 startpath();
 roundrect(0,0,100,100,30,30);
 endpath();
 fillandstrokepath();
 printwrapped("#NAME#");
}
```

Inheriting Tagged Values

Remember we used tagged values to store extra information about our applications? Like their ownership, functional fit, technical fit, and more?

There is a simple way to add these tagged values to the stereotype definition so it is easier to fill them out, and we don't forget any.

Here is how to do it:

1. Locate the stereotype definition in the toolbox diagram. It is called "software."

2. For each tagged value you want to add, add an attribute with the name of the tagged value (e.g., "Ownership"). Choose the appropriate type (such as "char" for a string) and give the attribute an initial value corresponding with the default value (e.g., "COTS" in the case of Ownership).

3. Export and import the toolbox. When you try it, you will see that the SEAM tagged values even get a separate tab "Systemplar::Software" next to the default tagged values.

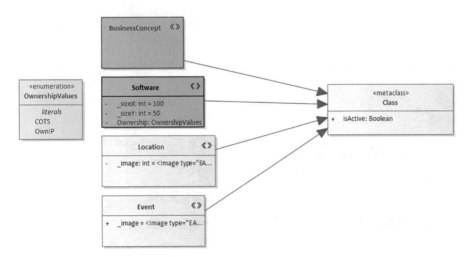

Figure 9-9. *The adapted toolbox definition*

We can even go a step further, by limiting the possible values of the "Ownership" tag. Here is the step plan (Figure 9-9):

1. From the Profile toolbox, add an element of the type "enumeration" to the diagram and call it "OwnershipValues."

2. Add two attributes to this element, one for each of the possible values (COTS and OwnIP).

3. In the Software stereotype, go to the attribute "Ownership" and click "Type" ➤ "Select Type." Navigate to the OwnershipValues element and confirm (Figure 9-10).

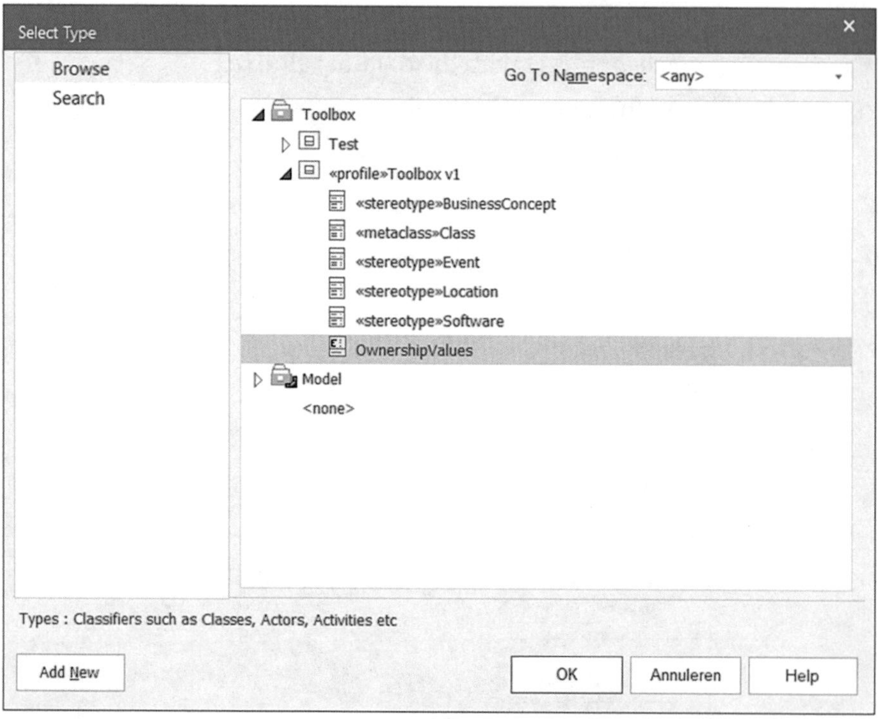

Figure 9-10. Select a type for the OwnershipValues

Tip   You can reapply a stereotype definition by dragging the stereotype from the toolbox in the resources window to the appropriate element on the diagram (Figure 9-11). The element will then update with all new information such as size definitions and tagged values. Colors and Shape Scripts will update automatically.

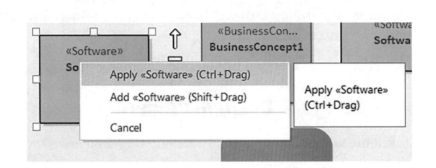

Figure 9-11. *Reapplying a stereotype*

Adding Diagram Properties

A special type of element properties is aptly called "diagram properties" because they apply to a certain element but only for the current diagram.

Suppose we want to tie our "events" list from the "timing" view to the processes. Events include "New Customer," "New Order," "Legal Change," and more. These can be seen as "triggers" for the processes. Sometimes, however, these triggers don't come nice and separate. For example, an order from a new customer is both a trigger for the process "onboard new customer" as for the process "service existing customer." But in the context of describing the general sales process, the "onboard new customer" process is only a side effect: we need to update our customer data in order to service this new customer. So the "main trigger" is still the "order" process.

221

On the other hand, if we are describing the "marketing" process, the "onboard new customer" process is the focus and "new customer" the "main trigger."

If we now want to make the "main trigger" stand out, we could of course just color it differently on the different diagrams. But there is a better way to achieve this, so that we can change our minds later (the color should be yellow instead of black) or that we could even add Shape Scripts to make it stand out even more clearly, without revisiting all of our diagrams.

We can use the concept of "diagram properties" here.

Step 1: Adding the Diagram Property

Add an attribute to the event stereotype with following contents:

- Name: MainTrigger

- Type: (empty)

- Scope: Public

- Stereotype: Diagram property (select "new" and create it if it does not exist yet)

- Alias: vMainTrigger

- Initial Value: 0

It is important to name the Alias and to name it differently from the diagram property name.

Step 2: Changing the Shape Script of the Event Stereotype

We will add this code to the existing Shape Script. It is easy to guess what it does:

```
if (HasProperty("vMainTrigger","1"))
 {
    setfillcolor(0,0,0);
    setfontcolor(255,255,255);
 }
```

The full code now reads like this:

```
shape main{
 noshadow=true;
 v_align="center";
 h_align="center";
 setfillcolor(150, 150, 150);
 if (HasProperty("vMainTrigger","1"))
 {
    setfillcolor(0,0,0);
    setfontcolor(255,255,255);
 }
 startpath();
 roundrect(0,0,100,100,30,30);
 endpath();
 fillandstrokepath();
 printwrapped("#NAME#");
}
```

Figure 9-12. A diagram property as a context menu item

Step 3: Updating the Existing Elements and Testing

Now we generate the toolbox, import it in the resources window, and reapply the stereotype "event" to the existing events "new customer" and "new order." Right-click any of the events and choose "MainTrigger" from the context menu (Figure 9-12).

Now any event that gets marked as "MainTrigger" will be colored black on the diagram instead of gray (Figure 9-13).

Figure 9-13. A diagram with a main trigger

Toolbox Visibility

A note on the visibility of toolboxes: As we discussed in Chapter 2, the diagram type steers the toolbox that will open by default when activating the diagram.

However, you can have some toolboxes open by default.

In the Toolbox window, click the button with the three horizontal bars. Scroll all the way down and select "Toolbox visibility." Select the appropriate toolbox and confirm with OK.

This works only for toolboxes that come with their own toolbox page. A full discussion of how to accomplish this is outside the scope of this book, but some useful guidelines can be found in the help (look for MDG Technology SDK) and in the list with resources that is included in the appendix of this book.

Epilogue

Level one of the framework defines the boundaries.

—John Zachman

Summary

In this final chapter, we saw how easy it is to create a custom toolbox and the advantages this offers. As said in the beginning of the chapter, there is a lot more to tell about creating toolboxes. Please see the resources and useful links in the appendix to learn more about this topic.

APPENDIX

Useful Resources

Since SparxSystems Enterprise Architect is a very open platform, there is ample opportunity to build on it. Many websites offer plug-ins and other extensions to the original platform, of which I have found four especially helpful.

LieberLieber

Peter Lieber and Konrad Wieland focus on three areas: model-based systems engineering, modeling infrastructure, and integration with Enterprise Architect from multiple other applications and tools.

`www.lieberlieber.com/en/home-en/`

Bellekens

Geert is one of the leading experts in Enterprise Architect. Name it, and he has done it. From setting up EA to document generation, scripting, to using different methodologies or developing custom add-ins... His website offers lots of free-to-use scripts, tips, and more.

`https://bellekens.com/`

Thomas Kilian

Another expert is Thomas Kilian. He has written several books about Enterprise Architect, each from a specific point of view such as scripting, shapescripting, the MDGs, or the EA database. Very pragmatic and to the point.

`https://liquit.biz/brain/books.html`

© Peter Doomen 2023
P. Doomen, *Introduction to SparxSystems Enterprise Architect*,
https://doi.org/10.1007/978-1-4842-9312-6

eaDocX

If you need Word or Excel documents out of your EA model, search no longer: eaDocX is the place to be. Their solution even includes round-tripping so you can import the documents back into EA.

www.eadocx.com/

Of course, there is also the website of SparxSystems itself, where you can find

- Updates and release notes including bug fixes.

- Webinar recordings detailing specific use cases for Enterprise Architect (and links to upcoming webinars).

- A bug reporting form (!).

- Tutorials and helpful information.

- A user forum where you can discuss anything related to Enterprise Architect, going from feature suggestions to "how-tos" to bugs and issues. As a regular user, you should create an account on this forum and visit it once in a while.

- Extensions and related products that might come in handy depending on your specific context.

https://sparxsystems.com/products/ea/

Index

© Peter Doomen 2023
P. Doomen, *Introduction to SparxSystems Enterprise Architect*,
https://doi.org/10.1007/978-1-4842-9312-6

E

Printed in the United States
by Baker & Taylor Publisher Services